Sutpen's Design

Interpreting Faulkner's

Absalom, Absalom!

SUTPEN'S DESIGN

Interpreting Faulkner's
Absalom, Absalom!

DIRK KUYK, JR.

University Press of Virginia
Charlottesville and London

THE UNIVERSITY PRESS OF VIRGINIA
Copyright © 1990 by the Rector and Visitors
of the University of Virginia

First published 1990

Library of Congress Cataloging-in-Publication Data

Kuyk, Dirk, 1934–
    Sutpen's design : interpreting Faulkner's Absalom, Absalom! / Dirk
Kuyk, Jr.
        p.   cm.
    Includes bibliographical references (p.)
    ISBN 0–8139–1260–1
    1. Faulkner, William, 1897–1962. Absalom, Absalom! I. Title.
PS3511.A86A6745   1990
813'.52—dc20   89-25109
                                                                       CIP

Printed in the United States of America

To Winkie,
to Mother,
and to Dirk

Contents

Acknowledgments   I am grateful for the help of five friends. Paul Smith, James A. Miller, James Wheatley, and T. J. Banks all read the manuscript and gave me good advice. Patricia J. Bunker, reference librarian in the Trinity College library, searched out books and journal articles and got them for me from three continents.

Sutpen's Design

Interpreting Faulkner's

Absalom, Absalom!

Prologue

THIS BOOK BEGAN in an undergraduate class on William Faulkner's
Absalom, Absalom! Because the students kept referring to "Sutpen's
design" without pausing to define it, I asked, "What, exactly, was
Sutpen trying to do?" They gave the answers that I expected.
They had, after all, read not only the novel but also some of the
criticism; and they had accepted, as I had, the basic account that
has been developed since *Absalom* was published in 1936. When I
asked for evidence to back up their answers, the students pointed
to passages that every critic would cite. Ordinarily, I would have
accepted the citations; this time, to make the students defend their
interpretations, I set out to challenge them—and discovered that
the passages fail to support the interpretations. When they collapsed, my interpretation also collapsed; it stood on the same
ground. So did all the criticism that I had read; it would also fall.

Now, after surveying virtually all the criticism of *Absalom*, I
have concluded that the account that forms the basis for that criticism is mistaken. This book argues that the account is flawed in
two crucial ways. It misunderstands both what Sutpen is trying to
do and how the narration works. As a result of the first misunderstanding the account fails to explain, for example, why Sutpen
rejects Bon and what Sutpen hoped for in striving to complete his
design. The second misunderstanding has led critics to see *Absa-*

lom as a web of hypothetical narratives that cannot be verified. Because the book's characters serve as narrators and are patently unreliable, critics have doubted that a trustworthy narrative can be derived from what we are given. I believe that the book's narrative technique reveals a way to authenticate the narrative. These ideas about Sutpen's design and about the narration lead to a detailed reinterpretation of *Absalom*.

Even a slight misreading embarrasses the critic. If *Absalom* has been misinterpreted continually for decades, as I contend, that fact might embarrass criticism itself, especially when we consider how much critics have come to admire the novel. Although its first reviewers looked at it askance, today *Absalom* towers among Faulkner's works; only *The Sound and the Fury* seems to approach its stature. Moreover, we can now hear it described as the greatest American novel of the century and as joining *Moby-Dick* and *Huckleberry Finn* at the pinnacle of American fiction. Critical esteem has been accompanied by sustained, serious critical attention. Freud, Burke, Cassirer, Barthes, and Derrida have all been brought to bear on *Absalom*. It has been related to the Faulkner canon, to the Bible, to southern history and American history, to various genres and subgenres—in short, almost every critical theory has offered its interpretation of the novel. If none of that critical effort has understood key aspects of *Absalom*, that fact may invite us to ask, If the best readers have failed, if they have been misled by their own assumptions and practices, what can their difficulties show us? Can we learn anything about how to avoid difficulties ourselves? Those are the broadest questions that I am considering here.

Sutpen's Design begins in the middle of *Absalom, Absalom!* and immerses its readers in the criticism. In doing so, *Sutpen's Design* may seem meant to speak only to Faulkner critics. Although they will doubtless make up much of its audience, I hope that the book will find two other kinds of readers. Those interested in the practice of criticism may read *Sutpen's Design* to examine how critical theories have been applied in interpreting *Absalom*. For those readers *Sutpen's Design* may serve as a case study of how critical approaches may fail and succeed. Finally, *Sutpen's Design* hopes for readers who are neither Faulknerians nor theorists but who have just read *Absalom* for the first time and wish to understand it better before reading it again. *Absalom, Absalom!* is, it seems, designed for rereading and for reinterpretation.

1
Sutpen's Design

"YOU SEE, I HAD A DESIGN IN MY MIND." In William Faulkner's *Absalom, Absalom!* that line occurs on page 329, more than two thirds of the way through the book.[1] Readers, eager or driven to press on, do not pause to think about it; but the line repays contemplation. By *design*, Thomas Sutpen certainly means a plan that he had conceived and had sought to carry out. *Design* might mean still more. Because Sutpen was seeking retaliation, *design* might imply a plan of attack: Sutpen might have formed a design *upon* someone or something. Whatever *design* means to Sutpen—and I think that his meaning is far from fully understood—his tone, as he speaks the line, expresses neither repentance nor bravado. Sutpen calls the design his own not as an admission or a claim but as a plain statement of fact. The coldness of his tone and his lack of shame and remorse have led many readers to condemn him. They may read *design* ironically, as if Sutpen is unknowingly condemn-

---

1. Subsequent quotations from *Absalom, Absalom!* are cited parenthetically in text. Quotations follow the 1986 edition, *Absalom, Absalom! The Corrected Text*. Earlier studies had to rely on the 1936 edition, which contained a few significant differences, particularly in the dates of events in the narrative. I have pointed out the differences that might have influenced a reader's interpretation. In quoting a writer who cited the 1936 edition, I have also given the 1986 citation, identifying it as *AA:CT*.

ing himself for a brutal, selfish scheme. Although *Absalom* is more than the story of Thomas Sutpen, readers strive to understand his acts and his aims because they lie in the book's core. We'll soon get back to his design; before we do, we need to look into some other implications of the sentence "You see, I had a design in my mind."

Sutpen's verb may be significant. Why does he use the past tense: "had"? Does he mean that he had his design but has given it up or that he still has it? The design was "in my mind"—does that mean that he had never gotten it embodied in the world? Does it mean that he had never even tried to express it until he sat down in General Compson's office and began his account? His opening words, "You see," fix his own roles and General Compson's. Sutpen is the teller; General Compson, the listener; but Sutpen is also the actor in the narrative. Unable to interpret his own story, he is turning to General Compson to interpret it for him. "You see" may not be simply a statement; it's almost a command.

And, indeed, many have sought to obey him—have tried to "see." Rosa was the first. General Compson struggled to do so and passed the challenge on to Mr. Compson, who passed it to Quentin, who shared it with Shreve. In 1957 and 1958 while writer-in-residence at the University of Virginia, Faulkner himself grappled with Sutpen's design not as the book's author but as one of its readers. Although he seldom seems to have reread his books, he found *Absalom* so demanding that he resorted to rereading it. Before then his comments had denigrated Sutpen, oversimplified Sutpen's design, and so misrepresented the book; but after rereading it, Faulkner said that the narrators had presented only partial truths. As Faulkner the reader then saw Sutpen, "the old man was himself a little too big for people no greater in stature than Quentin and Miss Rosa and Mr. Compson to see all at once. It would have taken perhaps a wiser or more tolerant or more sensitive or more thoughtful person to see him as he was."[2] Faulkner's words contain a warning that too few have heeded. Critics who have written on *Absalom* believe that Sutpen is quite transparent. They see him as petty and egocentric rather than as "too big," and they seldom seem to have felt that understanding him and his design calls for any special wisdom, tolerance, sensitivity, or thoughtfulness. But once we have grasped exactly what Sutpen's design was,

2. Gwynn and Blotner, 274.

we will see in it less self-serving ambition and more of an aspiration that might actually deserve the word *heroic*.

We will also find that Sutpen's design does not stand in isolation in *Absalom*. Other characters have their designs, not only plans that they seek to carry out but also schemes that they've formed to the detriment of others. We will try to understand their aims and motives and to comprehend how their designs mesh or fail to mesh with Sutpen's and with one another's. We will try to see whether their designs came to exist in the world or existed only in the characters' minds. And we will find many characters shifting among the roles of actor, teller, and listening interpreter in a chain that stops only with the reader as the last interpreter and with Faulkner—or, more precisely, *Absalom* itself—crying out, "You see."

"You see, I had a design in my mind," Thomas Sutpen said. How he came to form his design is clear. As a boy Sutpen had moved with his family from the Appalachian backwoods and had settled in a cabin on a plantation in Tidewater Virginia. When he was twelve or thirteen, his father sent him to the plantation house with a message for the owner. Sutpen knocked at the front door. The black butler, obviously carrying out his master's notions of propriety, told the boy "never to come to that front door again but to go around to the back." Sutpen, brought up under the egalitarian code of the mountains, was stunned. He went into the woods to a cave "where he could be quiet and think" (290). He knew "he would have to do something about it in order to live with himself for the rest of his life and he could not decide what it was because of that innocence which he had just discovered he had" (292).

Sutpen never considers vengeance against the black butler because Sutpen knows him to be merely the owner's instrument. Sutpen rejects the notion of killing the owner because "that wouldn't do no good" (293). Soon the boy decides that vengeance against the owner is pointless: "There aint any good or harm either in the living world that I can do to him" (297). Sutpen, with "that innocence instructing him" (297), suddenly finds his design taking shape in his mind:

'If you were fixing to combat them that had the fine rifles, the first thing you would do would be to get yourself the nearest thing to a fine rifle you could borrow or steal or make, wouldn't it?' and he said Yes. 'But this aint a question of rifles. So to combat them you have got to have what they have that made them do what he did. You got to have land and niggers and a fine house to combat them with. You see?' and he said Yes again. He left that night. (297)

. . . . .

I had a design. To accomplish it I should require money, a house, a plantation, slaves, a family—incidentally of course, a wife. I set out to acquire these. (329)

But by the time those words occur, some three hundred pages into the book, many other designs have impressed themselves on the minds of readers. That overlay of other designs has, I believe, kept readers from seeing precisely the design that Sutpen had in mind. Eventually I'll devote much attention to those other designs, trying to determine how they affect the ways readers have understood the book. Now, however, I'll keep focusing on Sutpen's design.

What do readers think Sutpen aimed to do? Let's see what critics have said. (The narrator in *Tom Jones* explicates the word *critic* by saying, "By this Word here . . . we mean every Reader in the World."[3] So do I. Therefore, the readers who publish their views will stand in here for all those who don't.)

Readers are essentially unanimous about the nature of his design. Elizabeth M. Kerr speaks for many of them when she says that Sutpen's "Grand Design" was "to establish an estate and a dynasty . . . on the Tidewater pattern of inheritance through the eldest legitimate son." Cleanth Brooks also finds Sutpen trying to "establish a dynasty." Being sent to the back door made Sutpen change the saying "if you can't beat them, you'd best join them" by adding "you can beat them only by joining them"; and so Sutpen "dedicated his life to becoming the Tidewater planter." David Paul Ragan says that Sutpen wanted to become, "like Pettibone, a participant in the power structure."[4]

Some critics stress still more that the design has its source in society because society admires those who build dynasties. Ilse Dusoir Lind says that Sutpen chose the "path of social conformity." Donald M. Kartiganer agrees: Sutpen's path leads him to

<hr/>

3. Fielding, 302.

4. Kerr, *William Faulkner's Gothic Domain,* 38; Cleanth Brooks, *William Faulkner: Toward Yoknapatawpha,* 293; Ragan, *William Faulkner's* Absalom, 112.

"self-imprisonment in a prevailing social system. . . . His quest is not to create a design, but to accomplish an already existing one, a pattern he can neither understand nor modify to suit himself." Olga W. Vickery writes that "the germ of Sutpen's design is simply his determination to create . . . that pattern which he sees, rightly or wrongly, in Southern society and to conduct his life strictly in terms of its ethical code."[5]

Other critics emphasize the psychic rewards Sutpen will achieve by building his dynasty. David Minter contends that Sutpen aims to "match or even surpass" the plantation owner's "power and grandeur" because Sutpen "wants to avoid the failure that marks his family, particularly his father." Minter says that what Sutpen does, "he does in part for himself, so that he can live with himself for the rest of his life; in part for his forbears . . . ; and in part for the boy he was, or more precisely, for the 'boy-symbol' that the boy he was has become."[6] John T. Irwin says: "Sutpen seeks revenge within the rules of patriarchal power for the affront that he suffered; he does not try to show the injustice of the system, but rather to show that he is as good as any man in the system. If the planter is powerful because he is rich, then Sutpen will have his revenge by becoming richer and more powerful than the planter. And he will pass that wealth and power on to his son, doing for his son what his own father could not do for him."[7]

This critical unanimity is odd in the light of what Sutpen actually accomplishes. Having formed his design, he moved with remarkable speed to carry it out. Knowing that "to accomplish my design I should need first of all and above all things money in considerable quantities and in the quite immediate future" (303–4), Sutpen went to the West Indies where, he had heard, "poor men . . . became rich" (302). There he worked as overseer on a plantation, put down a slave rebellion, and at the age of twenty married the master's daughter. When he married, he was "still a virgin. . . . that too was a part of the design which I had in my mind" (310). He grew wealthy and had a son. At this point he seems to have acquired absolutely everything called for in his design, as readers have usually understood it. He ought, then, to have rested easy.

5. Lind, 298; Kartiganer, *Fragile Thread,* 88; Vickery, 94.

6. Minter, *William Faulkner,* 154.

7. Irwin, 98.

Sutpen, however, repudiated his wife and child because "I found that she was not and could never be, through no fault of her own, adjunctive or incremental to the design which I had in mind, so I provided for her and put her aside" (300). Although a reader might join Estella Schoenberg in conjuring up notions that might account for Sutpen's putting his wife aside—for example, she might have been illegitimately pregnant, insane, illiterate, oversexed, or prone to fits[8]—almost all readers think, as I do, that he had discovered that his wife was partly black. (Eventually I will try to show why that fact or belief or even rumor would have impeded the design. But one seeming explanation might as well be dismissed now. Miscegenation itself would not defeat what readers generally take to be Sutpen's design. Racial mixing would not bar him or his wife from high status in the West Indies, and Sutpen himself did not object to it: Clytie seems to have been his daughter.) If he were aiming merely at establishing a dynasty and then "lying in his hammock in the shade, with his shoes off, receiving drinks brought to him by a servant,"[9] he seems not to have noticed that he has completed his design. Nor does the critics' view of his design seem to account for his decision to remain a virgin until his marriage. Abstinence is neither adjunctive nor incremental to creating a dynasty.

Sutpen's next steps might stir still more doubts about what his design was. Having come so close to its completion, he abandoned almost all that he had gained. He left his wife the plantation and all that went with it except twenty slaves and a sum of money, made his way to Jefferson, and began once again his effort to carry out his design. He bought one hundred square miles of virgin bottomland from the Chickasaws. With his slaves and a seemingly kidnapped and certainly imprisoned architect he built a mansion. By some scheme that Mr. Coldfield, a respectable merchant and Methodist steward, participated in but was ashamed to profit from, Sutpen furnished his mansion with "chandeliers and mahogany and rugs" (50). He married Coldfield's daughter, Ellen; and they had two children, Henry and Judith. Again he has laid the foundation for a dynasty and ought to be ready to recline in his hammock. His design, as the critics have described it, seems—for the second time—complete.

8. Schoenberg, 81–82.

9. Cleanth Brooks, *William Faulkner: Toward Yoknapatawpha,* 293.

Henry, the scion of the dynasty-to-be, came home for Christmas with a college friend, Charles Bon, from New Orleans. Henry idolized the older, more sophisticated Bon; but what attracted Bon to Henry? Sutpen himself seems to have wondered; and when the boys' friendship lasted through the spring, Sutpen undertook to investigate Bon's background. Mr. Compson's account emphasizes how uncharacteristically Sutpen was behaving: "Sutpen, the man whom, after seeing once and before any engagement existed anywhere save in his wife's mind, he saw as a potential threat to the (now and at last) triumphant coronation of his old hardships and ambition, of which threat he was apparently sure enough to warrant a six hundred mile journey to prove it— this in a man who might have challenged and shot someone whom he disliked or feared but who would not have made even a ten mile journey to investigate him" (125). Henry brought Bon home in June while Sutpen was away. With encouragement from Henry and from Mrs. Sutpen, Bon and Judith began a courtship. Sutpen, in the meantime, had discovered in New Orleans something about Bon. Expecting that Bon would know that he had been found out, Sutpen may have hoped that Bon would retreat. During the fall, however, the courtship continued; and Sutpen held his hand, again uncharacteristically for "this man of whom it was said that he not only went out to meet his troubles, he sometimes went out and manufactured them" (130). On Christmas Eve, Sutpen acted: he forbade the marriage. When Henry objected, Sutpen justified his decision by revealing something he had discovered in New Orleans. Henry, taking Bon's side, gave his father the lie; and the two boys left Sutpen's Hundred.

Sutpen's stand against the marriage is puzzling. What had he found in New Orleans? How had he justified his stand to Henry? Was the justification that Sutpen had offered his true reason for forbidding the marriage? And, most puzzling of all, why would Sutpen risk his design by estranging Henry in order to stave off the marriage?

A few readers dismiss efforts to answer such questions. Kartiganer, for example, writes that Sutpen withholds his consent "for some unknown reason."[10] Schoenberg goes further. She says that "the many critical attempts to establish the facts and the sequence of Sutpen chronology devolve from, and their errors are

10. Kartiganer, *Fragile Thread,* 93.

partially explainable by, the mistaken premises, first, that *Absalom, Absalom!* is primarily Sutpen's story and second, that the events of the Sutpen story are supposed to have happened. Even in terms of the text, not to say the author's intent, most of them either did not happen or cannot be proved to have happened." For her, Sutpen's story is "*im*material—literally," and so no one need bother trying to figure it out. Yet she undermines her own stand by arguing that Quentin carries the book's action by his "gathering of information, assimilating it, telling it, developing part of it . . . into an elaborate fictional narrative, and bringing his . . . personal involvement in the tale" to a high pitch.[11] Quentin, however, isn't unique in carrying out those acts. They describe pretty well what is done by Rosa, Mr. Compson, General Compson, and Shreve; by Faulkner as author; and by the book's readers themselves. Almost all critics have therefore tried to work out Sutpen's motives for barring the marriage. To do so turns out to be more difficult, I believe, than critics have suspected.

Let's take the first question first: What had Sutpen discovered in New Orleans? Mr. Compson told Quentin that Sutpen had found Bon's octoroon mistress and their son there (128). Perhaps Sutpen had even discovered that she and Bon had married in a non-Christian ceremony. Mr. Compson's view seems correct so far as it goes; but as he himself feels, it doesn't go far enough: "Granted that . . . the existence of the eighth part negro mistress and the sixteenth part negro son, granted even the morganatic ceremony—a situation which was as much a part of a wealthy young New Orleansian's social and fashionable equipment as his dancing slippers—was reason enough, which is drawing honor a little fine even for the shadowy paragons which are our ancestors born in the South and come to man- and womanhood about eighteen sixty or sixty one. It's just incredible. It just does not explain" (123–24). Mr. Compson's inability to work out a credible explanation frustrates him. Like Kartiganer and Schoenberg, Mr. Compson says that Sutpen, Bon, Judith, and Henry "dont explain and we are not supposed to know" (124). Unlike those critics, though, he doesn't give up. He imagines the four people as chemicals brought together by a formula incorrectly written or in an experiment improperly performed: "You bring them together in the proportions called for, but nothing happens; you re-read, te-

11. Schoenberg, 75, 135, 134.

dious and intent, poring, making sure that you have forgotten nothing, made no miscalculation; you bring them together again and again nothing happens" (124–25). With those remarks Mr. Compson prefaces his account of what Sutpen discovered and why that discovery led him to bar the marriage. That account has failed to satisfy readers as it failed to satisfy Mr. Compson himself. Sutpen, we think, must have found more than that.

But the reader must turn many pages before the narrative offers another explanation. It takes an unexpected form: it comes from Shreve, the narrator who stands furthest from the Sutpens. When Henry brought Bon home, Shreve says, Sutpen "looked up and saw the face he believed he had paid off and discharged twenty-eight years ago" (331). Quentin agrees and adds a good many comments that Mr. Compson had made about Sutpen and Bon as father and son. All of that surprises Shreve, who challenges Quentin: "Your father. . . . He seems to have got an awful lot of delayed information awful quick, after having waited forty-five years. If he knew all this, what was his reason for telling you that the trouble between Henry and Bon was the octoroon woman?" Quentin replies, "He didn't know it then"; and when Shreve asks, "Then who did tell him?" Quentin answers simply, "I did" (332). We have here the answer to our first question: Sutpen had discovered in New Orleans that Bon was his son.

Sutpen surely didn't tell Henry all about that during their Christmas Eve confrontation, however. Instead, what Mr. Compson surmised rings true: Sutpen told Henry that Bon had a mistress (possibly a wife) and a child in New Orleans. Mr. Compson's account of Henry's trip with Bon to see the octoroon in New Orleans also fits in with her visit to Sutpen's Hundred and with Clytie's and Judith's ability to find and to help Bon's son, Charles Etienne. Furthermore, when Mr. Compson was sitting on the porch telling Quentin about Sutpen, Mr. Compson had not yet learned who Bon's father was. Mr. Compson's ignorance is itself a faint indication that both Sutpen and Bon had kept Bon's parentage secret. Thus, the answer to our second question: Sutpen justified his decision to Henry by telling him about Bon's mistress (or wife) and child.

Two questions remain: Did Sutpen tell Henry the true reasons for forbidding the marriage, and why would Sutpen risk his dynasty to stave off the marriage? To the first of these questions my short answer is no, Sutpen had reasons he was keeping in reserve. Exploring what they were and why he was holding them back will make the second question puzzling and will bring to light more problems with the notion that Sutpen aimed merely at establishing a dynasty.

Let's return to the question of Bon's parentage. Almost all readers believe, as I do too, that Bon is Sutpen's son although, again, Schoenberg disagrees. The narrative, she says, contradicts the supposition that Bon is Sutpen's son. She rests her argument on two grounds. Bon's gravestone, which Judith ordered, shows Bon to have been born in New Orleans in December 1831. Schoenberg believes that if he were really Sutpen's son, the gravestone would give his birthplace as some island in the West Indies. Is that information wrong then, she asks, because of misinformation or because of subterfuge, Judith's or someone else's? Whatever the case, Schoenberg objects to the narrative's failing to state a motive or to explain how the inscription on the gravestone came to be wrong. While I can't conceive of Judith's sinking to subterfuge, the other possibilities are entirely plausible. And a motive is easy to imagine. Even though Bon was keeping quiet about his origins, he would have to have given himself some background. Bon, then, would be the source of this information. He may have believed it himself; he may not have. No matter which, I see no "contradictions" there. Schoenberg also asserts that "nowhere in the multiple telling of Sutpen's story by those who could know is there evidence that even Sutpen thought Bon his son."[12] I hope to offer such evidence with Sutpen himself as the witness, but I must still develop the case before bringing Sutpen to the stand.

Although readers do join in taking Bon as Sutpen's son, they quickly separate on exactly why that fact makes Sutpen forbid the marriage. Hyatt Waggoner merely says that Sutpen "could calculate no advantage to be gained by recognizing Bon as his son, and [Sutpen] was not one to be moved by the incalculable."[13] Most critics, though, expend more effort than that in working out the calculations that Sutpen was making. Quentin and Shreve explore the possibility that Sutpen prevents the marriage to prevent incest. But like Quentin and Shreve, most readers find that explanation insufficient. No one regards Sutpen as so appalled at the prospect of incest that he would feel he must stop the marriage at any cost.

12. Schoenberg, 80–81.

13. Waggoner, 166.

Indeed, the critics seldom discuss incest as an impediment to Sutpen's plans. I agree: he is pursuing his design so bullheadedly that a little incest wouldn't give him pause.

By far the majority of readers conclude that Sutpen bars the marriage because Bon's mother had "a tinge of Negro blood" and Bon is therefore partly black. Lind says, "The slight fraction of Negro blood, whose denial was Sutpen's crime, is sole cause. Now at last we know what turned father against son." Vickery finds that "Sutpen must choose between his adherence to the concept of pure blood and his own and his son's humanity." The reason for his having to make that choice might seem self-evident: as Gerald Langford says, "Bon's Negro blood was clearly a threat to the establishment of a dynasty in the antebellum South." [14]

Langford would be indubitably right if Sutpen had meant to found a dynasty on Bon. Since southern culture took "partly black" as "entirely black," no white dynasty could rest on Bon. But Henry, not Bon, was Sutpen's foundation stone. Therefore, Bon's existence would not inherently imperil Sutpen's design if it were simply to found a dynasty. Brooks explains why:

> In view of what is usually written about *Absalom, Absalom!,* the basic security of Sutpen's position needs to be stressed. Suppose that it had become known, either through Sutpen's action or Bon's, that Bon was his son; what, in view of the laws and customs of the time, could Bon have done? He might have created a certain amount of talk. . . . But with [Sutpen's] hundred square miles of plantation and his respectable marriage to Ellen Coldfield, Sutpen could probably have outfaced any charge of bigamy, and by letting the community know that Bon was part-Negro, could have disposed of any notion that Henry was not his legitimate heir. [15]

One could probably make that argument still more strongly. If Sutpen's first wife was partly black, then in Mississippi at the time the marriage would have been illegal. Sutpen could not have made it valid even if he had wished to. Nor could he have in any way legitimized Bon as the child of such a marriage.

14. Longley, "Thomas Sutpen," 118; Lind, 288; Vickery, 96; Langford, 9.

15. Cleanth Brooks, *William Faulkner: Toward Yoknapatawpha,* 298.

Does Langford perhaps mean that Bon's marriage to Judith would threaten the Sutpen dynasty? If people knew either that Bon was partly black or that Bon was Sutpen's son, then, of course, the miscegenation or the incest would make the marriage both illegal and taboo. But who would discover and reveal either of those bits of information? Bon had grown up as not only a white but an upperclass, wealthy white in the sophisticated city of New Orleans; he was studying law at the university (which, one hardly needs to say, admitted no blacks); and no one appears to have doubted his mother's race or his father's name. And, indeed, one might wonder whether a dynasty in a patriarchal society would fall because of a daughter's and sister's scandalous behavior, no matter how great the scandal. In sum, I believe, Brooks's judgment stands: Charles Bon's racial heritage does not threaten the security of Sutpen's dynasty.

Irwin offers an intricate psychological explanation for Sutpen's rejecting Bon: "In the ideal situation, the revenge is inflicted on the same person who originally delivered the affront . . . ; in the other situation, the revenge is inflicted on a substitute. This second situation sheds light on Sutpen's attempt to master the traumatic affront that he suffered as a boy from the man who became his surrogate father, to master it by repeating that affront in reverse, inflicting it on his own son Charles Bon."[16] Irwin's explanation would make the rejection of Bon the fulfillment of Sutpen's design, the achievement of his revenge by delivering the affront to the surrogate. But Irwin's explanation leaves too much unexplained. Sutpen learned in the spring that Bon was his son. Why, then, would Sutpen, who kept driving single-mindedly toward his goal, wait until the following Christmas to get his revenge? Why not complete his design instantly? And once had had rejected Bon, why didn't he get at least a moment's satisfaction from attaining his vengeance and completing his design? Sutpen's own words, passed from General Compson through Mr. Compson to Quentin, undermine Irwin's explanation. Sutpen said that if he were forced to play his "last trump card"—that is, to take the action that definitively rejects Bon—"I destroy my design with my own hand" (341–42). Sutpen's words virtually contradict the idea that rejecting Bon gains Sutpen the revenge that fulfills his design.

16. Irwin, 116–17.

Occasionally a critic finds in primogeniture rather than race the reason that Bon poses a problem for Sutpen. For example, Kerr says, "Sutpen himself chose to adopt the laws of primogeniture and refused to recognize Charles Bon, his legitimate elder son and rightful heir by those laws."[17] Of course, as we've already seen, if people regard Bon as black, then those laws would preclude Bon as either a legitimate son or a rightful heir. But what happens if people take Bon as white? John T. Matthews answers that question by saying that Bon imperils "Sutpen's insemination of a legitimate line. . . . Sutpen cannot acknowledge Charles Bon without accepting a world in which origin and priority have lost their privilege, in which rival sons claim the same father, differing signs the same signified. Sutpen refuses one son and remains loyal to the false authority of dynastic speech."[18] Yet if Sutpen seeks merely to found a dynasty, then his plight is not so grave as that. Fraternal rivalries are just the kinds of conflicts that "dynastic speech" came into being to resolve. Dynastic speech always stands ready to decide questions of origin and priority. It would have to name the rightful heir; but whether it chooses Henry or Bon, Sutpen would still have a foundation for his dynasty.

We have reached a crux. Although we know that Sutpen forbade the marriage, we have eliminated all the widely held reasons for his doing so. He does not seem to have acted to prevent incest. Miscegenation neither offended him nor threatened a dynasty founded on Henry; and primogeniture would have allowed him to found his dynasty on whichever son was his "rightful" heir. Why, then, did he forbid the marriage? What in the world was Sutpen trying to do?

Now it's time to call Sutpen himself to the witness stand so that we can hear him explain his design. His testimony—or, more accurately, my account of his testimony—must pass this test of credibility: it must answer all the questions, large and small, that the standard interpretations don't answer.

> —In Haiti why did Sutpen give up just as he had succeeded
>   or had nearly succeeded in completing his design?
> —Why did Sutpen regard his virginity as important to his
>   design?

17. Kerr, *William Faulkner's Gothic Domain*, 39.

18. Matthews, 157.

—Why did Sutpen forbid the marriage?

—Henry killed Bon after the end of the Civil War. In the previous year, however, we heard Sutpen saying that he would have to choose between two courses that would lead to "the same result." We understand, I believe, his first course. If he plays his "last trump card" by telling Henry about Bon, then he expects Henry and Bon to fight. If Henry dies, the Sutpen dynasty will have lost its foundation. If Bon dies, Henry will vanish, as he does, in despair because he will have slain his friend and half brother. All that, Sutpen foresees. But what are we to make of his second course? To take it, he would "do nothing, let matters take the course which I know they will take and see my design complete itself quite normally and naturally and successfully to the public eye, yet to my own in such fashion as to be a mockery and a betrayal of that little boy who approached that door fifty years ago" (342). In this course Bon and Judith would marry; and Henry, kept ignorant that Bon was his half brother, would accept—even welcome—the marriage. The dynasty would go forward. The public eye would regard the design as successful. So would the standard critical interpretations. Why, then, would Sutpen regard this course as a "mockery and a betrayal"? If he were seeking only a dynasty, why wouldn't he then have his design complete and unchallenged?

Scattered throughout *Absalom,* Sutpen's remarks reveal much about his design. They call for a close reading that can begin with the rifle analogy that his "innocence" uses to instruct him as his design is coming into being. His innocence teaches him that someone who means to "combat" men with fine rifles would try to get himself "the nearest thing to a fine rifle" he could (297). Since Sutpen means to make his dynasty his weapon, he must have a "fine" dynasty—that is, a dynasty as nearly perfect as possible. The standards of perfection are, of course, not Sutpen's alone; they are the standards of society. Without wealth a family can't deserve the name *dynasty;* therefore, Sutpen would, as he says, "require money, a house, a plantation, slaves." A dynasty must extend beyond a single generation: Sutpen would thus "require . . . a family." Since in the society the children must be legitimate, Sutpen would "require . . . incidentally of course, a wife" (329). His family must include a son under patriarchal primogeniture.

Meeting those requirements would not suffice to make a dynasty fine. In Sutpen's place and time those requirements are merely the dynasty's defining traits. A fine dynasty, like a fine rifle, must surpass an ordinary one. Again, the standards are the society's. If society sees blacks as inferior to whites, then a fine dynasty cannot be black. If society regards part-black as entirely black, then neither husband nor wife can be partly black. If society regards, say, an olive skin or even a rumor of blackness as suspicious, then a fine dynasty cannot rest on such suspect foundations. And if female—and male—virginity are seen as extraordinarily admirable, then the man who founds the finest dynasty will be a virgin. Sutpen is trying to create "the nearest thing" (297) he can to a fine dynasty.

Yet the rifle analogy is not grounded in mere possession. One doesn't combat men with rifles simply by having similar rifles nor even by having better rifles. No, to use a rifle to combat riflemen, one fires the rifle at them. Sutpen's design, then, must go beyond just having the rifle, beyond just having what the plantation owner had, even beyond having more than he had. If Sutpen aims to have a dynasty, he must also aim to "fire" it at someone.

Who—or what—would he take as his target? Not the black butler or the plantation owner who turned him away. Virtually from the start Sutpen was aiming elsewhere. Again, his analogy itself clarifies his intention. He would have wanted a fine rifle to combat "them that had the fine rifles"; he must have wanted a fine dynasty to combat those who had fine dynasties. The analogy may help us take the next step, too. In fighting those with fine rifles, a man who has gotten a fine rifle would fire it. But how might one use a dynasty against those who have dynasties? How does one fire a dynasty at a dynastic society?

We are now reaching what I take to have been Sutpen's design. He meant, I believe, not merely to acquire a dynasty but to acquire it so that he could turn it against dynastic society itself. And he meant to do that in an ironic, perhaps even a doubly ironic, way. Quentin repeats for Shreve and for us what Sutpen told General Compson about the design. Because the two boys are, by this time in the book, probing the relationship between Henry and Bon, not inquiring into Sutpen's design, neither Quentin nor Shreve comments on or even seems to notice the meaning of Sutpen's remarks. And few readers seem to have given the passage the attention it deserves. Here is the passage in full with some comments along the way.

> The design.—Getting richer and richer. It must have looked fine and clear ahead for him now: house finished, and even bigger and whiter than the one he had gone to the door of that day and the nigger came in his monkey clothes and told him to go to the back, and he with his own brand of niggers even, which the man who lay in the hammock with his shoes off didn't have, to cull one from and train him to go to the door when his turn came for a little boy without any shoes on and with his pap's cutdown pants for clothes to come and knock on it.

Sutpen is establishing his dynasty in preparation for the moment when "his turn" will come for a little boy to knock on his door. When the boy knocks, the butler will go to the door to do whatever Sutpen has trained him to do. Sutpen may seem to be preparing to reenact his own rejection by inflicting it on a boy who symbolizes the young Sutpen. Quentin, however, tells a different story:

> Only Father said that that wasn't it now, that when he came to Grandfather's office that day after the thirty years, and not trying to excuse now anymore than he had tried in the bottom that night when they ran the architect, but just to explain now, trying hard to explain now because now he was old and knew it, knew it was being old that he had to talk against: time shortening ahead of him that could and would do things to his chances and possibilities even if he had no more doubt of his bones and flesh than he did of his will and courage, telling Grandfather that the boy-symbol at the door wasn't it because the boy-symbol was just the figment of the amazed and desperate child.

In the last couple of clauses Sutpen is describing himself as "the amazed and desperate child"crouching deep in thought in his cave in the woods. There he had imagined the "boy-symbol" or "figment" representing himself at the door. He must have also imagined himself as a man opening the door or having his butler open it on his behalf. But that figment, that vision, stemmed only from the boy's amazement, desperation, and youth. The boy-symbol "wasn't it." The boy-symbol at the door was not the design. Instead, Sutpen said

> that now he would take that boy in where he would never again need to stand on the outside of a white door and knock at it: and not at all for mere shelter but so that that boy, that whatever nameless stranger, could shut that door himself forever behind him on all that he had ever known, and look ahead along the still undivulged light rays in which his descendants who might not even ever hear his (the boy's) name, waited to be born without even having to know that they had once been riven forever free from brutehood just as his own (Sutpen's) children were. (325–26)

That is Sutpen's design. He required "money, a house, a plantation, slaves, a family—incidentally of course, a wife" (329)—not for themselves, not because they'd enable him to lie in a hammock with his shoes off, not for the social status they'd provide, but so as to be ready for the knock on his door. And when the boy, "that whatever nameless stranger," knocked, Sutpen meant to "take that boy in." Sutpen planned to give him more than "mere shelter"; Sutpen meant to take him into his own family. The boy could then "shut that door himself forever behind him" on his past and look into the future toward his descendants—and not just toward a share in the riches of a Sutpen dynasty. In describing the aim of his design, Sutpen looks beyond wealth and power and status and sees lines of children, the boy and his descendants, "riven forever free from brutehood just as his own (Sutpen's) children were."

The rifle analogy, not yet stretched quite to its breaking point, may serve us one last time. To return the fire of those with the fine rifles, one shoots back. The similar rifle fires in the opposite direction. The plantation owner had the little boy turned away; Sutpen will open the door and welcome the "nameless stranger" into his family. The dynastic society's bullet had struck the boy Sutpen with such tremendous force that Sutpen the man has never recovered. As he draws a bead on dynastic society, Sutpen aims to fire back the highest-velocity bullet he can. He wants his return shot to strike with maximum impact.

Yet since he knows that the society wears armor to protect itself, he must design a bullet that will pierce that armor. If he

lacks money, a house, a plantation, and slaves when he opens the
door, his bullet would be a dud. To invite the boy in to have a
share of little or nothing would seem meaningless to dynastic society. Sutpen's act would not bear on it at all. If he's wealthy but
lacks a family, dynastic society would explain his act away by saying something like "You can't take it with you. No wonder he
took in that ragamuffin. He needed somebody to take care of him
in his old age, and he can keep him there by promising to remember him in his will." If Sutpen's wife is partly black, society would,
as we've seen, judge their union to be illegal and taboo. To open
the door to a white boy and invite him into such a household
would, in the eyes of society, be to besmirch the status of even a
nameless stranger. If Sutpen's wife is even rumored to be black,
society would use the rumor to protect itself against the significance of Sutpen's act. If he has a family but no son, dynastic society would still shield itself with "When he dies, his name will
vanish. He had to take that boy in. Sutpen needed an heir." In
sum, then, Sutpen must have everything that dynastic society admires so that, when he opens the door and takes the boy in, society will be unable to snatch up any fact or rumor and take shelter
behind it. The bullet he has designed will then strike home.

Sutpen's design would free the boy and his descendants forever from the backwoods brutehood in which Sutpen grew up and
from which he raised himself. Yet in shaping that design, Sutpen
remains faithful to his innocent boyhood belief in what we might
call an egalitarian noblesse oblige. In Tidewater Virginia he had
learned that

> there was a difference between white men and white men
> not to be measured by lifting anvils or gouging eyes or
> how much whiskey you could drink then get up and walk
> out of the room. That is, he had begun to discern that
> without being aware of it yet. He still thought that that
> was just a matter of where you were spawned and how;
> lucky or not lucky; and that the lucky ones would be even
> slower and lother than the unlucky to take any advantage
> of it or credit for it, feel that it gave them anything more
> than the luck; that they would feel if anything more tender
> toward the unlucky than the unlucky would ever need to
> feel toward them. (282)

From the start, then, Sutpen meant his design to teach society the lesson that those lucky enough to have risen above brutehood should at least care about the feelings of the unlucky. Through his design Sutpen would not just preach this lesson but teach it by his own example. He would reach down and lift up one of the unlucky, a little boy, a nameless stranger knocking at his door. He may have imagined that the people lucky enough to have power would witness his opening the door, feel shame at their own hardheartedness, and change their ways. (But if his design had succeeded, those people would not, I suspect, have understood it any better than, say, most readers have. Sutpen's trouble was, indeed, innocence.)

For Sutpen as a boy even to conceive of such a design required a powerful act of imagination. His conception did not spring from the traditional source of such ideas: from the Christian maxim "Love thy neighbor as thyself" exemplified in such stories as that of the Good Samaritan. Sutpen's upbringing seems to have been without religion. Nor did the conception simply grow out of Appalachian egalitarianism. While the mountain people he came from would never have sent a caller around to the back door and might have been "tender toward the unlucky" (282), taking a nameless stranger into the family surely would have lain beyond their ken. The design, of course, reaches even further than that. Sutpen intends to free the stranger's descendants from brutehood forever and, by doing so, to strike at the heart of the patriarchical structure on which not only the southern plantation but also Western culture itself had been based. That is the conception, the design, that sprang full-grown from the boy's mind.

If conceiving the design is a triumph of the imagination, Sutpen's single-minded effort to carry it out is an impressive act of determination. Rosa and the Compsons and Shreve and the people of Yoknapatawpha look on not only in puzzlement but in awe. And so, I think, should we as we watch a man bound by time and caught in the flux of events dare to imagine the design and then dare to try to consummate it.

In another sense, too, the design is an anomaly. Faulkner was writing the book in the 1930s, in the midst of the depression. Plenty of nameless strangers were knocking at front doors. Many were sent round to the back. Householders might offer a meal in exchange for a chore or give the stranger a handout, but few considered taking the stranger in and freeing him and his descendants from brutehood forever. (The social legislation of the New Deal, however, might be said to spring from a conception a little like Sutpen's.)

Readers who accept this view of Sutpen's design will find their experience of reading *Absalom* considerably altered. They will, rightly, continue to object to his using other people as objects to put in place, ready for the knock at the door. Yet although his means of completing his design remain ruthless and wrong, his end is now seen not as selfish aggrandizement but as an attack on the immorality of dynastic society. *Absalom* may, then, call upon us to answer the question that Mr. Compson, speaking of Judith, asks Quentin: "Have you noticed how so often when we try to reconstruct the causes which lead up to the actions of men and women, how with a sort of astonishment we find ourselves now and then reduced to the belief, the only possible belief, that they stemmed from some of the old virtues? the thief who steals not for greed but for love, the murderer who kills not out of lust but pity?" (150).

As we'll see in more detail later, this view of Sutpen's design authenticates some of the narrators' observations that otherwise seem inappropriate. Rosa, for example, senses that Sutpen stands larger than life even though she comprehends nothing of his design except that she believes, according to the third-person narrator, that it was to be an "assault upon . . . respectability" (42); and Mr. Compson conceives of Sutpen as a figure of irony and tragedy. We may share Mr. Compson's feelings as we read Quentin's account of the moment in which Sutpen heard the knock, opened the door, and

> "Henry said, 'Father, this is Charles' and he . . . saw the face and knew that there are situations where coincidence is no more than the little child that rushes out onto a football field to take part in the game and the players run over and around the unscathed head and go on and shock together and in the fury of the struggle for the facts called gain or loss nobody even remembers the child nor saw who came and snatched it back from dissolution;—that he stood there at his own door, just as he had imagined, planned, designed, and sure enough and after fifty years

the forlorn nameless and homeless lost child came to knock at it and no monkey-dressed nigger anywhere under the sun to come to the door and order the child away; and Father said that even then, even though he knew that Bon and Judith had never laid eyes on one another, he must have felt and heard the design—house, position, posterity and all—come down like it had been built out of smoke, making no sound, creating no rush of displaced air and not even leaving any debris. (333)

That account contains two kinds of irony. What its narrators, Quentin and Mr. Compson, are saying has dramatic irony. Although neither of them has perceived the essence of Sutpen's design, their analysis of his feelings is true, but true in a way beyond their comprehension. They imagine that Sutpen foresees only the fall of his dynasty; but as he himself says to General Compson, he has also foreseen another possibility—an ironic success. For the "coincidence" that brings Bon to the door is itself ironic: Sutpen cannot open the door to him as a nameless stranger because Bon is his son.

Sutpen recognizes his own plight. Seeing himself caught in that ironic dilemma, he goes to General Compson to review his actions and to discuss the dilemma. Sutpen begins by framing the questions he wants to answer: "You see, I had a design in my mind. Whether it was a good or a bad design is beside the point; the question is, Where did I make the mistake in it, what did I do or misdo in it, whom or what injure by it to the extent which this would indicate" (329). Next, he sketches the way his dilemma arose out of his marriage in Haiti.

I had a design. To accomplish it I should require money, a house, a plantation, slaves, a family—incidentally of course, a wife. I set out to acquire these, asking no favor of any man. I even risked my life at one time, as I told you, though as I also told you I did not undertake this risk purely and simply to gain a wife, though it did have that result. But that is beside the point also: suffice that I had the wife, accepted her in good faith, with no reservations about myself, and I expected as much from them. . . . I accepted them at their own valuation while insisting on my own part upon explaining fully about myself and my pro-

genitors: yet they deliberately withheld from me the one
fact which I have reason to know they were aware would
have caused me to decline the entire matter, otherwise they
would not have withheld it from me—a fact which I did
not learn until after my son was born. (329)

Sutpen's words here allow readers to begin inferring his reason for
setting his first wife aside. The Haitian family had "deliberately
withheld" a fact that, if revealed, would have made him refuse the
marriage. Sutpen's context—"I [explained] fully about myself and
my progenitors; yet they . . ."—implies that his wife and her parents had deliberately withheld a fact about her progenitors. The
fact is, furthermore, one that revealed itself when the baby was
born and, as Sutpen will soon add, precluded the woman and the
child from having a part in his design. The likeliest inference: Sutpen saw the baby, grew suspicious, questioned his wife or her
parents, and learned that she was partly black. (Incidentally, although a few readers have thought that Sutpen might have set
aside his wife because her baby was not his, Sutpen's phrasing here
contradicts that. He says unequivocally "my son.")

Although the marriage had cost him "wasted years," he had
sought an annulment that would be more than just; and his wife
had agreed to it. "I made no attempt to keep not only that which
I might consider myself to have earned at the risk of my life but
which had been given to me by signed testimonials, but on the
contrary I declined and resigned all right and claim to this in order
that I might repair whatever injustice I might be considered to
have done by so providing for the two persons whom I might be
considered to have deprived of anything I might later possess: and
this was agreed to, mind; agreed to between the two parties"
(330).

We have already heard Sutpen call his Haitian wife's baby
"my son." Now Sutpen thinks himself ready to look ahead across
the "more than thirty years" between that time and the moment
when Bon stands at the door. Later Sutpen will say that the dilemma he faces with Bon at the door devolved out of his situation
in Haiti (342). Sutpen's own words provide each of those bits of
evidence; and all those bits, linked together, support most readers'
belief that Sutpen knows Bon to be his son.

But before Sutpen can move to his present dilemma, he feels
obliged to recapitulate his previous difficulty. (At the ellipsis be-

low, Quentin breaks off quoting Sutpen. The ellipsis represents a ten-page digression in Quentin's narrative but no gap, I believe, in Sutpen's.)

> And yet, and after more than thirty years, more than thirty years after my conscience had finally assured me that if I had done an injustice, I had done what I could to rectify it—. . . I was faced with condoning a fact which had been foisted upon me without my knowledge during the process of building toward my design, which meant the absolute and irrevocable negation of the design; or in holding to my original plan for the design in pursuit of which I had incurred this negation. I chose, and I made to the fullest what atonement lay in my power for whatever injury I might have done in choosing, paying even more for the privilege of choosing as I chose than I might have been expected to, or even (by law) required. (330 and 341)

For himself—and for General Compson—Sutpen is obviously reconfirming that he has treated his first wife at least justly. On discovering the hidden fact, he had faced a painful choice. He sets out the options he had. (A flaw in parallel structure clouds his meaning. Faulkner probably intended to contrast *condoning* with *holding,* but the word *in* before *holding* throws the two gerunds out of balance.) The first of Sutpen's options was to stay with his wife and their new son on the Haitian plantation. To have taken that option would have "meant the absolute and irrevocable negation" of his design. If his design were merely to create a dynasty, his statement would make no sense; but, as we've seen, his statement is consistent with a design that leads up to opening the door and taking in the nameless stranger. So he takes his second option— "holding to my original design"—and sets his wife aside.

His recapitulation complete, Sutpen is ready to pick up the line of thought that he began with: "And yet, and after more than thirty years." Here are the words with which he describes his dilemma at finding Charles Bon at his door: "Yet I am now faced with a second necessity to choose, the curious factor of which is not, as you pointed out and as first appeared to me, that the necessity for a new choice should have arisen, but that either choice which I might make, either course which I might choose, leads to the same result" (341). We might take the word *faced* literally. In Haiti, Sutpen must have realized he had to make his first choice when he looked at the baby's face. Now, looking at that face again, he sees that he must choose again. But this time he knows that either choice he makes will prevent him from completing his design. Nevertheless, he does have a choice: he can choose either of two ways to fail. His first alternative: "Either I destroy my design with my own hand, which will happen if I am forced to play my last trump card . . ."(341–42). This is the choice he eventually makes. He plays his last trump when he tells Henry enough to drive him to kill Bon, go into hiding, and remove himself as the foundation of the dynasty. Actually, Sutpen slightly overstates the case here. Although he appears to foresee what Henry will do, Sutpen doesn't realize that he himself will make two more attempts—with Rosa and Milly—to father a son and thus once again stand ready to complete his design by opening the door to the stranger. Reestablishing his design does remain possible; all he needs is another son qualified to be his heir. Still, Sutpen is essentially right; for despite his tenacity he will never again stand ready to answer the nameless stranger's knock.

If Sutpen were seeking no more than a dynasty, then the first alternative would plainly be fatal to his design. His second alternative, however, would appear to complete it, as he himself says. He might either play his last trump card "or do nothing, let matters take the course which I know they will take and see my design complete itself quite normally and naturally and successfully to the public eye" (342). That is, he will have the public effect he is seeking if he allows Bon and Judith to marry and takes Bon fully into his family. Again, I think, he overstates. If he were, say, to make Bon co-heir with Henry, the public eye might widen a bit with surprise. Sutpen would be displaying uncommon generosity for a father-in-law—and less than common sense in a society in which primogeniture preserves large holdings from fragmentation. But merely to surprise people would hardly satisfy Sutpen; he is more likely to be aiming a blow at the public eye. But even if his second alternative were to have the public effect his design seeks, Sutpen would nevertheless reject it. He would know its effect to be a fraud. His design would complete itself to the public eye and "yet to my own in such fashion as to be a mockery and a betrayal of that little boy who approached that door fifty years ago and was turned away, for whose vindication the whole plan was conceived and carried forward to the moment of this choice, this second choice devolving out of that first one" (342). Critics who believe that Sutpen seeks only a dynasty have scanted this part of Sutpen's explanation, which makes their view untenable. Judith's and Bon's marriage would have been unlikely to disturb the dynasty in any way and surely not in a way that would mock and betray the little boy. But if the design calls for getting everything ready to open the door to the nameless stranger, Sutpen cannot open it to Bon. Bon is disqualified for half a dozen reasons; but for Sutpen, I think, the first five don't count. First, Bon isn't nameless (although he doesn't bear his father's name). Second, since he's Henry's friend and college classmate, he is not a stranger. Next, at thirty years of age he's no little boy. Nor is he impoverished as Sutpen had been when he knocked at the plantation house door. (In fact, Bon seems roughly as well-to-do as Sutpen himself.) Fifth, since Bon is or might be partly black, Sutpen couldn't legally take him openly into the family. (He might be included covertly as Clytie and Charles Etienne were, but that kind of inclusion would not suffice in fulfilling the design.) Those five disqualifications, strong as they may be, would not deter Sutpen, I believe; but the sixth does. Sutpen cannot open the door and take Bon in because Bon is his son. The father has an obligation to his son—an obligation, by the way, that Sutpen believes he has already kept. Sutpen's design calls for his accepting someone to whom he has no societal obligations whatever. Therefore, to open the door and take his own son into the family would indeed be "a mockery and a betrayal" to Sutpen's eye, no matter how the public eye viewed it. Sutpen therefore rejects his second alternative and begins telling Henry more and more until Henry kills Bon.

2

Designs of the Narrative:

The Narration
and
the Fabula

ABSALOM DOES NOT STRIVE to make Sutpen's design easy to see. The other characters do not seem to understand what he is doing. They are busy with designs of their own, plans they seek to accomplish—and sometimes schemes they intend to carry out to the detriment of others. But before we investigate their designs, we need to examine the way *Absalom* enshrouds all the characters' designs in multiple narration. The narration seems to have succeeded more in concealing than in revealing Sutpen's design. The narrators who are southern cannot understand it through any conventional southern paradigm; indeed, Sutpen created his design precisely to shatter such paradigms. And Shreve, the Canadian who stands apart from those paradigms, nevertheless lacks a model for comprehending what Sutpen sought to do. Therefore, what is typical in multiple narration is true in *Absalom:* its narrators make untrustworthy guides.

But if we want to hear the story at all, we have no choice: we must listen to them. Yet as they speak, our minds inevitably go to work. We infer and imagine; we try to discover facts and to gauge probabilities. And as we do so, we come to notice that the narrators build their accounts on their own knowledge, inference, and imagination and color those accounts according to their own assumptions, desires, antipathies, and perhaps even aesthetic preferences for one kind of narrative or another. Thus we find that the narrators have their own designs, designs not only as intentions and possibly schemes but also as the patterns that the narrators use to shape their accounts. To discover facts and to gauge probabilities, we try to peer beneath and beyond all those kinds of designs. Out of the narrators' accounts we too build narratives colored by our own assumptions, desires, antipathies, and aesthetic preferences. And so we readers have our own designs, our own patterns that we use to try to find meaning. *Absalom* thus is a palimpsest of designs—plans, schemes, and narrative patterns—imposed by characters, narrators, readers, and, I probably need not add, Faulkner himself.

This chapter begins the tracing and analysis of these layers of designs. Ideally, the neatest way to proceed would be to trace and analyze each layer separately. The book's multiple narration, however, makes that impossible. Because the narrators sometimes disagree about the characters' motives and actions, one can't always separate the layer of the characters' designs from the layer of the narrators' designs. Consequently, this chapter will confront those disagreements and evaluate each narrator's account.

This chapter attempts to answer only the basic questions about how the narrators came to know the story and about why they are recounting it. This chapter won't go beyond those "factual" issues to pursue the ways in which the narrators color their accounts. And yet, as we know, the line between fact and coloring is always finally imaginary. For example, Rosa's desire to make her narrative melodramatic influences how she reports events and even what events she chooses to report. Nevertheless, this chapter will stop at that imaginary line so that we can establish the book's *fabula*—that is, a chronological outline of the major acts of the book. The fabula will contain dates and acts, will identify the narrator who gives the date, and will comment on discrepancies between narrators' accounts. Chapter 3 will draw on the fabula in exploring the other characters' designs, and then chapter 4 will return to the narrators to investigate how they color their accounts according to their own assumptions, desires, antipathies, and aesthetic preferences.

The Narrators

Since we are about to consider the narrators almost as if they are historians, we might well heed a warning from David Levin's *In Defense of Historical Literature:*

> The mistake of most commentary on Faulkner's use of history in this novel has been to assume that a prejudiced or erroneous historian is a discredited historian. The process by which we move from Miss Rosa's angry images to Mr. Compson's more humane analysis, and then to the discovery of several important errors in Mr. Compson's interpretation, shows us—requires us as we read to carry on—the practices by which history is created and understood. Historical error is inevitable, but every narrator must venture an explanation, and almost every human explanation has some value that persists even after the interpretation has been superseded.[1]

If narrators have taken part in the story they are telling, their own experience makes a most reliable source; but a couple of generations lie between the years of the Sutpens' story and 1909–10, when Rosa, Mr. Compson, Quentin, and Shreve do their narrating. Nevertheless, quite a bit of *Absalom* consists of narrators telling what happened to them. Rosa tells of the Sutpens' carriage racing to the church on Sundays, of visiting Ellen at Sutpen's Hundred, of arriving there after Bon's death, of her own attitude toward Bon's courting, of her feelings when Judith barred her from the room where Bon lay dead, of waiting for Sutpen to return from the war, and of his return, their engagement, and her rejecting him. Her remarks about Sutpen's appearance and behavior draw some authority from her having known him. Quentin's narration depends far less on his own experience: he tells of the quail hunt when he saw the Sutpen's gravestones and of his and Rosa's visit to Sutpen's Hundred. Mr. Compson's narration draws little from his own experience; and Shreve's, of course, nothing at all.

If one wants to know about an event one hasn't seen, one may seek witnesses. All four narrators do so frequently. Rosa reports,

---

1. Levin, 134–35.

for example, what she has learned from Ellen and Mr. Coldfield. Mr. Compson has acquired eyewitness information from his parents. Both General and Mrs. Compson attended Sutpen's and Ellen's wedding, and General Compson was the man to whom Sutpen chose to tell his own story. Quentin has gotten information from Rosa, and Shreve constructs his narrative with what he has learned from Quentin. We hear from some witnesses only once. A coon-hunter named Akers claims to have walked up one of Sutpen's slaves out of the mud like an alligator (40); from Percy Benbow comes the story of the betting tickets his father kept in his law office in a file labeled "Estate of Goodhue Coldfield" (266). Such characters enter the book to convey only a bit of information, and then they are gone.

In addition to that fairly small group of witnesses whose names we know, the narrators use reports from many whose names we never hear. These witnesses sometimes also convey single bits of information—Mr. Compson, for instance, tells Quentin that Sutpen, passing through Jefferson, paused "only long enough for someone (not General Compson) to look beneath the wagon hood" and see that the wagon was full of slaves (40). The narrators draw together information from so many unnamed witnesses that one might imagine everyone in Jefferson engaged in observing the Sutpens. People watch the Sutpens for a couple of reasons. First, in a small town like Jefferson people naturally keep track of their neighbors and their doings. Second, Sutpen and his family stand out as both grandiose and enigmatic; they invite observation and analysis. Mr. Compson touches on both reasons at once as he begins to describe how Jefferson reacted when Sutpen first arrived: "In the next four weeks . . . the stranger's name went back and forth among the places of business and of idleness and among the residences in steady strophe and antistrophe: *Sutpen. Sutpen. Sutpen. Sutpen*" (35). Chapter 2 of *Absalom* reveals how the townspeople's observations and analyses flow together. The narration keeps citing the sources of its information with phrases like "the town learned later" (35), "Quentin's grandfather saw" (36), "it was years later before even Quentin's grandfather . . . learned" (37), and the townspeople "were certain" (38). Men ride out to Sutpen's Hundred, watch Sutpen and the black men working and hunting, and ride back to town to report and speculate on what they have seen. Their accounts, the narrative says, engender "the legend of the wild men" (40). When Sutpen's house stands completed but unfurnished for three years, "the town and the county watched him with more puzzlement yet. . . . now it was the women who first suspected what he wanted" (44). A myriad of observations and analyses enable the townspeople to form and test their inferences about their neighbors in general and the Sutpens in particular. Out of that process arises what is called common knowledge, the set of information, assumptions, and beliefs that the community takes to be true. In an interior monologue Quentin, speaking of himself, describes how having this common knowledge affected him: "But you were not listening, because you knew it all already, had learned, absorbed it already without the medium of speech somehow from having been born and living beside it, with it, as children will and do: so that what your father was saying did not tell you anything so much as it struck, word by word, the resonant strings of remembering" (266). The narrators often rely on common knowledge, which serves them in their narratives as it serves us every day. Common knowledge is, in particular, the bedrock for Mr. Compson's accounts, whether of Rosa (9–13, 70–79) or of the Sutpen family (49–69, 77–107, 109–63).

The narrators, too, make inferences and test them. Like historians—indeed, like anyone trying to interpret anything—they develop hypotheses from their own experience and that of others and from common knowledge. Rosa, who uses inference the least, infers that "something" has been living hidden in the house at Sutpen's Hundred (216). Mr. Compson, Quentin, and Shreve use inference extensively. We can see some of the signs of inference at work in these phrases from Mr. Compson's narration on pages 110 through 112:

> he must have realized
> He must have said . . . and must have repeated
> what else could he have hoped to find in New Orleans, if
>   not the truth?
> I can imagine him
> so Henry must have believed
> He may even have known
> he must have known
> I dont think she ever . . . suspected
> since doubtless he refused

The further the narrators stand from the events they seek to comprehend, the more they must rely on inference. From time to time *Absalom* itself explains how its narrators go about inferring the story they are telling. Inference is sometimes "ratiocination," an almost mathematical working-out of consequences. While that sort of inference may be necessary, *Absalom* scorns it as rigid and unimaginative. Quentin's and Shreve's room at Harvard is "dedicated to that best of ratiocination which after all was a good deal like Sutpen's morality and Miss Coldfield's demonising—this room not only dedicated to it but set aside for it and suitably so since it would be here above any other place that it (the logic and the morality) could do the least amount of harm" (350). But when inference and imagination join to construct a coherent and convincing narrative out of personal experiences, witnesses' reports, and common knowledge, then *Absalom* is lavish with its praise. For when Quentin and Shreve, still in their cold room, are beginning to find the missing elements in what Mr. Compson called the "chemical formula" (124) for the Sutpens' story, *Absalom* then says:

> All that had gone before just so much that had to be overpassed and none else present to overpass it but them, as someone always has to rake the leaves up before you can have the bonfire. That was why it did not matter to either of them which one did the talking, since it was not the talking alone which did it, performed and accomplished the overpassing, but some happy marriage of speaking and hearing wherein each before the demand, the requirement, forgave condoned and forgot the faulting of the other— faultings both in the creating of this shade whom they discussed (rather, existed in) and in the hearing and sifting and discarding the false and conserving what seemed true, or fit the preconceived—in order to overpass to love, where there might be paradox and inconsistency but nothing fault nor false. (395)

Narrators remember their experiences, observe facts, hear the reports of witnesses, and draw on common knowledge in making inferences. Those inferences are the narrators' efforts to sift and discard the false and to conserve what seems true. (The idea of "fitting the preconceived" looks ahead to a point I'm postponing until chapter 4.) Still, for *Absalom* all that amassing and sifting of facts and observations and common knowledge and ratiocination amounts only to the raking up of the leaves; the mutual act of imagination lights the bonfire.

The narrators, like the passage itself, recognize that the bonfire may blaze despite paradoxes and inconsistencies in their narratives. Rosa has told Quentin, in Shreve's phrasing, that "there are some things that just have to be whether they are or not, have to be a damn sight more than some other things that maybe are and it dont matter a damn whether they are or not" (403). Mr. Compson, too, does not stop creating his narrative when he finds it "incredible. It just does not explain" (124); he simply keeps trying. And Quentin and Shreve are indefatigable in striving to create a coherent narrative; and, by and large, they succeed. Of course, they do not ever interpret Sutpen's design although they have in hand all the evidence they would need to understand it. They take another path. Quentin and Shreve—fascinated by Bon's, Henry's, and Judith's feelings for one another—concentrate on them.

In fact, in at least one sense, all four of these narrators succeed: they get done what they aimed to do. Rosa told her story to get Quentin to accompany her to Sutpen's Hundred, and he did so. Mr. Compson was bringing together the elements in the chemical formula one more time; his account gave Quentin much of what he needed to make the formula work. Shreve gets the exciting story he wanted—and more. And Quentin, who had found in the Sutpen story something he "could not pass" (215), finally succeeds in working out why Henry killed Bon. Again, I'll carry this further in chapter 4; but now we ought to look at another basic question: Who counts as a narrator?

Oddly enough, critics have not agreed on who the narrators are. The four characters we've dealt with so far certainly count. Some critics—Irwin, for instance—stop with them. Other critics, like Kartiganer, add Sutpen since chapter 7 devotes a good many pages to quoting Sutpen's own accounts of his experiences and attitudes (299, 300–304, 310, 329–30, and 341–42). Of course, we hear Sutpen's words indirectly: he had spoken them to General Compson, who passed them on either to Mr. Compson or directly to Quentin. Nevertheless, since nothing suggests that this mediation has distorted what Sutpen said, I certainly count him as a narrator although his words do reach us through a line of Compsons.

A few readers, I imagine, might wish to exclude Sutpen as a narrator precisely because of that mediation. But that wish, if granted, would lead to a possibly surprising consequence. If we were to count as narrators only those whose words are unmediated, then Rosa, Mr. Compson, Shreve, and Quentin would themselves cease to be narrators. There is, after all, a third-person narrator, to whom critics have paid little attention. Every word in *Absalom* comes to the reader through that third-person narrator whose voice, like a continual hum, is hard to hear because it is omnipresent. We therefore ought to examine the narratives of Sutpen and the third-person narrator.

Sutpen's is quickly dealt with. He founded his design on common knowledge, the Appalachian belief in equality; but apart from that he speaks almost entirely from his own experience. He tells part of his story to General Compson to pass time during the hunt for the French architect and tells the rest of the story to give General Compson the background necessary for answering the question "Where did I make the mistake . . . ?" (329).

The third-person narrator has immense powers of perception and expression. Only a few critics have examined this narrator: Richard Forrer praises the narrator's "stabilizing and clarifying sense of reality," and Hugh M. Ruppersburg calls the narrator "a summarizing, unifying observer" who "both frames and visualizes."[2] The first few pages of *Absalom* give us a chance to notice many of the ways in which this narrator shapes the narrative as we hear it. The well-known opening paragraph with its long sentences, rhetorical structures, and bizarre figures of speech comes to us in that narrative voice. There the narrator reports the scene as an eyewitness: "Miss Coldfield . . . sitting so bolt upright in the straight hard chair that was so tall for her that her legs hung straight and rigid as if she had iron shinbones and ankles, clear of the floor with that air of impotent and static rage like children's feet" (3–4). Yet the narrator has the historical perspective to know that she has kept the blinds closed for forty-three summers because in her childhood she had heard that the dark is always cooler. The narrator can also look into the future: "It would be three hours yet" (9).

The narrator can report what Quentin is thinking and even give us the conversation of "two separate Quentins now talking to

2. Forrer, 30; Ruppersburg, 96.

one another in the long silence of notpeople in notlanguage" (5). The narrator can reveal, too, what the townspeople know. More than that, by saying that "none knew" (3) why Rosa still wears black, the narrator demonstrates the power to survey everyone's knowledge. The narrator can tell us things about Henry that only Henry can know: "Nor did Henry ever say that he did not remember" (443).

Judging the characters is another of the narrator's functions. It is the narrative voice that says that Quentin "did not recognize" Rosa's handwriting "as revealing a character cold, implacable, and even ruthless" (7). From the start the narrator even knows the outlines of the Sutpen story in at least three versions: as Rosa usually tells it (4), as Quentin recites it to himself (5–6), and as the town has inherited it (9).

While reporting every word of *Absalom,* the narrator also continues to set scenes, report common knowledge, convey characters' thoughts, make judgments, and look forward and backward. As a consequence much of what seems to reach us only from the characters who narrate gets authenticated by the third-person narrator as well. The fabula will show this narrative voice as the reader's source of information about many acts. That voice is the first we hear in every chapter except one; Rosa seems to speak without mediation in chapter 5 until, on the last of its 34 pages, the third-person narrative voice manifests itself. The immense power of this narrator becomes fully evident only as *Absalom* nears its end. By giving a little extra attention to its last three chapters, we can observe how the narrator reveals greater and greater powers of perception and expression.

In chapter 6 the narrator, like a film editor, glues together snippets of this and that into a continuous and coherent montage. The narrator's voice

—sets the scene in the room at Harvard and introduces Mr. Compson's letter telling Quentin that Rosa has died (217);
—gives the text of the letter (217–18);
—reports Quentin's and Shreve's remarks that launch their night-long reconstruction of the Sutpen story (218);
—reveals that the coming discussion won't be the first time that the roommates have gone over that story and reminds us that Quentin has never been able to "pass"

something in the relationships among Henry, Judith, and
Bon (218–19);

—reports Shreve's summary of what Quentin has told him
and what Shreve has inferred from that (The narrator also
reports Quentin's remarks confirming Shreve's inferences
[219–27]);

—reports Quentin's interior monologue, which Shreve obviously doesn't hear (Quentin's thoughts about how Sutpen died stem from information he has gotten from
observations and comments from the midwife and generally from townspeople [227–34]);

—reports Shreve's asking Quentin to tell him again about
the visit to the Sutpen graves (234);

—narrates the story directly, in the third-person, instead of
allowing either Quentin or Shreve to tell it and adds, unbidden, an account of the career of Charles Etienne
(While quoting Mr. Compson at length, thereby bringing
in information from General Compson and from inference, the third-person narrator also draws upon what the
townspeople think and records an interior monologue of
Quentin's, one in which Quentin expresses confidence in
his own powers of inference: "If I had been there I could
not have seen it this plain" [238]) (234–59);

—reports Mr. Compson's mention of Bon's letter that Judith had given to General Compson's wife (259);

—reports an interior monologue in which Quentin infers
what might have happened when Judith spoke with
Charles Etienne after his marriage (259–61);

—reports Mr. Compson's inferences, based partly on his
previous inferences and partly on common knowledge,
about Judith and Charles Etienne, about their deaths, and
about Clytie's raising Jim Bond (261–63);

—reports Quentin's interior monologue about how Judith's
gravestone got carved and erected, his information coming from Rosa by way of Judge Benbow and the townspeople's talk (Quentin's monologue also gives more of his
memories—of the visit to the graves and of another visit
when he and some other boys were frightened [263–69]);

—reports Shreve's saying that Quentin has told him that
Rosa had said that someone other than Clytie and Jim
Bond was living at Sutpen's Hundred (269–70).

The third-person narrator manipulates all this diverse material subtly, making unexpected connections and revelations, sometimes answering questions before the reader has thought to ask them and withholding other answers to let the suspense build. Most critics have spoken of these last three chapters as if Shreve and Quentin were the narrators, but even my sketch of chapter 6 shows not only the third-person narrator at work but also a narrative whose controlled complexity lies beyond the reach of either young man.

In chapter 7, which is equally complex and equally controlled, the third-person narrator, while remaining ever-present, recedes so that Quentin seems to carry most of the weight of the narrative. The bulk of his information comes from General Compson, who learned much of it from Sutpen himself. Through General Compson, Quentin can quote Sutpen directly. In fact, of the 239 lines that Sutpen speaks in *Absalom*, 197 occur in this chapter. While Quentin has witnessed little of the action he is recounting, he is composing a historical rather than a fictional narrative. When, for example, he tells how Sutpen rejected Milly and how Wash struck Sutpen down with a scythe, killed Milly and the baby, and was himself killed, Quentin is describing acts that occurred thirty years before he was born. His narrative, on pages 350 to 365, weaves together evidence from Mr. Compson, General Compson and his wife, the boy who found Sutpen's body, the midwife who delivered the baby, Major de Spain, common knowledge, and Quentin's own inferences. In this chapter the third-person narrator gives Quentin free rein and lets his narrative run. Yet even a narrator's silence can prove meaningful. By declining to qualify Quentin's account, the narrator lets it stand and thus, I think, authenticates it.

In chapter 8 the third-person narrator's power reaches its apex. Shreve's is almost the only voice in the cold room, Quentin having grown quiet. Shreve is working from inferences he has drawn from what Quentin has told him; and although Quentin speaks only six lines in the chapter's sixty-two pages, the narrator reveals that Shreve speaks for Quentin. They have joined in this act of imagination, and the narrative bonfire is blazing. The narrator says that Quentin and Shreve, while reimagining the Christmas confrontation at Sutpen's Hundred, identify so closely with Henry and Bon that the room at Harvard comes to contain "not two of them but four" (367). Two pages later the narrator, describing how Henry and Bon rode away in the Christmas dawn, repeats the identification: "Not two of them there and then either but four of them riding the two horses through the iron darkness."

The third-person narrator takes an unusual stance when Shreve is talking about Bon's mother and the lawyer. After reconfirming that Quentin and Shreve are still "both thinking as one," the narrator undermines their account by saying that they are "creating between them, out of the rag-tag and bob-ends of old tales and talking, people who perhaps had never existed at all anywhere" (378–79). A few critics—Schoenberg, for example—have extended this comment to apply to all the Sutpens; but that breadth of application is, I believe, mistaken. The context of the remark—that is, its occurring at this point in Shreve's account—should probably limit the application to the mother and the lawyer. Whatever the remark means, it demonstrates that the narrator will rein in Quentin's and Shreve's narratives rather than let them run unchecked.

After the "bonfire" passage that expresses approval of the boys' inferences (395), the third-person narrator changes the equation by which Quentin and Shreve identify themselves with Henry and Bon. Now, the narrator says, the four have become two: "Charles-Shreve and Quentin-Henry" (417). The change lasts only a moment here; on that page and the next they are four again. But their empathy with the account they're constructing plainly alters as they proceed.

The narrator then resumes evaluating their account—now, however, relinquishing the overt control employed in chapter 6. The drawing room "which Shreve had invented" as the setting for Henry's meeting with Bon's mother "was probably true enough." And the mother herself, "the slight dowdy woman with untidy gray-streaked raven hair coarse as a horse's tail . . . whom Shreve and Quentin had likewise invented . . . was likewise probably true enough." Mr. Compson had inferred that Bon had taken Henry to visit the octoroon. The narrator concurs, saying that "Bon may have, probably did" (419). And the narrator finds Quentin and Shreve "probably right" in their estimate of how Henry responded to that visit (420). The narrative voice, restricting its power to the evaluation of inferences, is now entering more than ever before into creating a narrative that must be "true enough" rather than just arranging reports of events. The bonfire of imagination is blazing higher.

The flames will soar, though, late in the chapter as the narrator's grip on the narrative grows stronger. The narrator interrupts Shreve just after Shreve has surmised that Henry, not Bon, had been wounded at Shiloh. Shreve's account has been vivid, with dialogue as well as action; nevertheless, the third-person narrator breaks in and distances us from their account by saying, "First, two of them, then four; now two again" (431). Although Shreve and Quentin go on talking, the narrator will no longer let us hear them. Instead, for most of pages 431 and 432 we can hear only the narrator's voice describing the room and the boys and summing up the last years of the Civil War as the Confederate armies fall back. The "two, four, now two again" recurs on page 432, but this time the second "two" refers not to Quentin and Shreve but to Bon and Henry: "the one who did not yet know what he was going to do, the other who knew what he would have to do yet could not reconcile himself." Within a few lines, though, the phrase refers once more to Henry and Shreve, "the two the four the two facing one another in the tomblike room." No longer does the narrative voice speak unobtrusively. Now the narrator compels our notice by whipping our attention back and forth.

Suddenly on page 433 the typeface changes from roman to italic. The book's momentum must often sweep readers along so swiftly that they pass the change without noticing it. But even readers who pause to notice may not find the meaning of the change immediately clear. The italic text has dropped all the topics that Quentin and Shreve have just been discussing and is taking up a new one, Bon's situation as the war ends. Does the new topic itself lead to the change? Probably not: new topics have arisen in the last few pages without new typefaces. Is there a new narrator? The account, which begins with a parenthesis and in mid-sentence, often infers Bon's thoughts but can sometimes quote them. Since the preceding passage, in roman type, was the third-person narrator's and since this one is also in the third-person, who else might be narrating it? Quentin? Shreve? Henry? For several pages one simply can't tell. The unidentified narrator says that Sutpen's regiment joined with Bon's and Henry's, that Bon "put himself in Sutpen's way" to give him a last chance to acknowledge Bon as his son, and that Sutpen's eyes revealed "no flicker, nothing" (435). Bon then decides that "that was all of it now and at last." When Henry realizes that Bon finally means to marry Judith, we hear them speak: "And then Henry would begin to say 'Thank God. Thank God' panting and saying 'Thank God . . . Dont try to explain it. Just do it' and Bon: 'You authorise me? As her brother you give me permission?' and Henry: 'Brother? Brother? You are the oldest: why do you ask me?' and Bon: 'No. He has never acknowledged me. He just warned me. You are the brother and the son. Do I have your permission, Henry?' and Henry: 'Write. Write. Write'" (436–37 [italics omitted]). That is vivid dialogue for a climactic moment. One might imagine an omniscient narrator—except that an omniscient narrator would probably have used the simple past tense, "began," rather than the modal verb "would begin" in the first line.

A few lines later the roman type resumes. Shreve is talking about another topic, the night when Rosa and Quentin went to Sutpen's Hundred. He goes on for a page and stops. The third-person narrator says: "It was just as well, since he had no listener. Perhaps he was aware of it." Quentin's thoughts lie elsewhere. What the narrator then adds needs careful reading: "Then suddenly [Shreve] had no talker either, though possibly he was not aware of this." That is, neither boy is talking; neither is telling the story. "Because now neither of them was there. They were both in Carolina and the time was forty-six years ago, and it was not even four now but compounded still further, since now both of them were Henry Sutpen and both of them were Bon, compounded each of both yet either neither" (438–39). They are so compounded that none of the narrator's earlier terms—"two," "four," and "Charles-Shreve and Quentin-Henry"—now suffices. Next, in midsentence, at the word *bivouac,* the italics return and continue to almost the end of the chapter: "smelling the very smoke which had blown and faded away forty-six years ago from the *bivouac fires burning in a pine grove, the gaunt and ragged men sitting or lying about them, talking not about the war yet all . . . facing the South*" (439). The narrator has shifted from the past tense into a series of present participles and, again, some modal verbs. And then the narrator changes tense again. The change, buried in the middle of another paragraph, may not at first catch one's eye:

"*The men about the fires would not hear this exchange, though they would presently hear the orderly plainly enough as he passes from fire to fire, asking for Sutpen and being directed on and so reaches the fire at last, the smoldering log, with his monotonous speech: 'Sutpen? I'm look-ing for Sutpen' until Henry sits up and says, 'Here'*" (439–40). From the past the narrative has moved to the present. Using verbs in the present tense, the third-person narrator is describing the action as it occurs. *Absalom* has brought the past to life.

The account in italics, which run unbroken from page 439 to 447, does not depend on any character's experience, observation, or inference but comes directly from the third-person narrator. Therefore, no other passage in the book can attain greater reliabil-ity than this account, which confirms some important details and casts new light on others:

—Sutpen says to Henry, "*You were hit at Shiloh, Colonel Wil-low tells me*" (441). Shreve's surmise was correct.

—Sutpen's saying "*I have seen Charles Bon*" (441) confirms Bon's belief that Sutpen had intentionally refused to ac-knowledge him.

—Elsewhere Sutpen's words have reached us through Gen-eral Compson, Mr. Compson, and Quentin. Now all those intermediaries are gone; the third-person narrator is reporting Sutpen's words at the moment he is speaking them. We therefore know exactly what he said that made Henry kill Bon: "*He must not marry her, Henry. His mother's father told me that her mother had been a Spanish woman. I believed him; it was not until after he was born that I found out that his mother was part negro*" (443).

—When Henry returns from meeting his father, Bon again asks, "*And he sent me no word? . . . No word to me, no word at all?*" A word of acknowledgment from Sutpen "*now, today,*" and Bon would give up his design to marry Ju-dith. He says, "*He didn't need to tell you I am a nigger to stop me. He could have stopped me without that, Henry*" (445). From the tense of Bon's verb Henry realizes that Bon has reached his decision. And, for Henry, Bon's decision makes his own inevitable. As Bon himself points out, "*I'm the nigger that's going to sleep with your sister. Unless you stop me, Henry*" (446).

When the italics end, Shreve is talking. Here his words mesh with the third-person narrator's account. For the first time Shreve calls Bon "black" (448), indicating that the two boys have reached the conclusion that the narrator has just discovered. The narrator then reports Shreve's justification for Bon's removing Judith's picture from the case she had given him and inserting the octoroon's and their child's: "It was because he said to himself, 'If Henry dont mean what he said, it will be all right; I can take it out and destroy it. But if he does mean what he said, it will be the only way I have to say to her, *I was no good; do not grieve for me.*' Aint that right? Aint it? By God, aint it?" (448). Quentin says, "Yes," and the chapter ends with the two boys and the third-person narrator in agreement.

Quentin's and Shreve's narratives, recorded by the third-person narrator, had raked up the leaves. That narrator, piling them thicker and thicker, was gradually drawn into the act of mutual imagination, until, almost by spontaneous combustion, the third-person narrative itself caught fire and blazed out of *was* into an incandescent *is*.

Two other readers have touched on how the narration authenticates the book's climax. Albert J. Guerard says: "Quentin and Shreve are actually carried back—the novel, rather, is carried back—to what I think is historical fact. They suddenly, with the italics on page 346 [*AA:CT* 433], partake of real omniscience."[3] *Omniscience* may be too sweeping a term. Quentin's and Shreve's "omniscience" is limited to the climactic scene. They apparently cannot, for example, see things that have interested them at least as much—for example, whether Judith and Charles loved one another. Still, Guerard is making a crucial observation: the novel's narrative reaches "historical fact." Thomas E. Connolly credits the third-person narrator with "magically translating" Quentin and Shreve to Carolina where they can "become witnesses to the scene and hear the voice that narrates the single most important piece of information in the novel. . . . Faulkner was unwilling to entrust this crucial information to either of these fallible narrators."[4] The words *become witnesses* and *hear* make Quentin and Shreve sound too much like an audience for the narrator. Yet even if another

3. Guerard, *The Triumph of the Novel*, 75.

4. Connolly, "Point of View," 271.

phrasing might be a little more faithful to the tone of the last pages of chapter 8, Connolly recognizes that Quentin and Shreve have attained the insight that the narrator has communicated to us.

This recognition of the third-person narrator's role may end the long debate over whether we readers actually know that Bon was black. Many critics have concluded that Quentin and Shreve merely imagined that he was because the boys felt that it makes the most coherent story. A few critics, among them Cleanth Brooks in *The Yoknapatawpha Country* and *Toward Yoknapatawpha and Beyond,* have striven to show that Henry told Quentin. Herschel Parker has argued that Quentin inferred Bon's race from seeing Jim Bond; Peter Brooks has argued that Quentin based the inference on seeing Clytie.[5] Either inference or both of them might have led to Quentin's (and thus to Shreve's) insight, but the text doesn't specify how Quentin attained it. For *us,* however, the text does authenticate it through the third-person narrator.

In chapter 9 the flames are still blazing vigorously at first, as the chapter describes Quentin's and Rosa's visit to Sutpen's Hundred. After a couple of pages of initial repartee between Quentin and Shreve, it's the third-person narrator, not Quentin, who tells the story we hear. Quentin seems not to be saying anything to Shreve while the narrator describes, in both third-person narrative and Quentin's interior monologue, how Quentin experienced the visit. Yet when that thirteen-page description ends on page 465 and we find Shreve speaking again, his topic, Rosa's return to Sutpen's Hundred to take Henry away in the ambulance, flows from it. The three imaginations are still running parallel to one another. Shreve's topic then leads naturally into the narrator's next description where, in a third-person account but without interior monologues, the narrator tells what Quentin imagines to have taken place when Rosa and the ambulance men neared the house and it burned down. Again, when that account ends, Shreve is speaking; and again his words fit in with the narrator's. In a few sentences he tries to conclude the story, but now the flames of imagination are guttering out. The three imaginations are drifting apart, even ceasing to function. The third-person narrative retires to its basic task of reporting. When Shreve asks, "Do you want to know what

5. Cleanth Brooks, *William Faulkner: Yoknapatawpha Country,* 436–37, and *William Faulkner: Toward Yoknapatawpha,* 322–28; Herschel Parker, 323–26; Peter Brooks, 258–59.

I think?" Quentin replies, "No"; and when Shreve challenges him to "tell me just one thing more. Why do you hate the South?" Quentin says, repeatedly, "I dont hate it" (471). Perhaps that's true; perhaps it isn't. I'll get back to that issue later. Whatever the case, the fire of mutual imagination is now dead.

The Fabula

The framework for discussions of the motives and actions of the characters in a novel is usually its plot. The word *plot* here means the story line in the order of its narration. In one sense *Absalom* presents its plot over and over again—three times, for example, in the book's first five pages. In a more important sense, however, the multiple narration prevents our using plot as a framework because the order of narration is nearly irrelevant to any determination of who did what when and why. The accounts conflict with one another and contain gaps. Since plot won't serve our purposes, we construct an alternative framework, the fabula of *Absalom*. The fabula arranges the acts of the book in chronological order. In interpreting any narrative, readers construct its fabula so that they can determine causes, consequences, and motives. I'll therefore outline the fabula of *Absalom*.

Other readers have naturally tried to do that, too. As Floyd C. Watkins has shown in "What Happens in *Absalom, Absalom!*," the gaps and the conflicts in the narrators' accounts often keep readers from knowing exactly what happened or from definitively dating it and leave them able only to try to assess what is most likely. Faulkner himself added to the difficulty by appending to *Absalom* a Chronology and a Genealogy that he put together hurriedly at his editor's request as the manuscript was going, chapter by chapter, to the printer. Both appendixes, although brief, often fail to match undisputed facts in the novel itself. The following fabula draws its dates and acts directly from the novel and ignores discrepancies between the novel and the appendixes. On the other hand, the fabula explores discrepancies among the narrators.

The Fabula *of* Absalom, Absalom!

1807

| About January | Thomas Sutpen born. | We learn from General Compson (by way of Quentin) that Sutpen himself didn't know his age "within a year on either side" (283). Quentin and Shreve calculate that since Sutpen was 25 when he arrived in Jefferson, he was born in 1808 (275). But evidence from the narrators who should prove more reliable about the birthdate points to his having been born earlier. Rosa confirms his age on his arrival (16) but says that he was 54 in the spring of 1861 (98) and 59 when he returned from the war in January 1866 (200). The third-person narrator says that "the town learned later" that Sutpen was "about twenty-five" on his arrival there (35). |

1817

| | Sutpen's family moves from the mountains to Tidewater. | Sutpen told General Compson that the Sutpen family had left the western Virginia mountains when Sutpen was 10 (279). |
| October 9 | Ellen Coldfield Sutpen born. | This data comes from her gravestone (236). Sutpen himself had it made. |

1821

| | The plantation owner turns Sutpen away. Sutpen forms his design and sets out on his quest. | According to General Compson, Sutpen said he was "just fourteen" when he "set out into a world which even in theory . . . he knew nothing about, and with a fixed goal in his mind" (62). |

1821 OR 1822

Sutpen goes to the West Indies.

Drawing—perhaps loosely here—on General Compson's accounts of his talks with Sutpen, Quentin tells Shreve that Sutpen was "fourteen or fifteen" when he went to sea in 1823 (299).

1827

Sutpen puts down the siege on the West Indian plantation where he has become overseer.

Reporting General Compson's account, Quentin quotes Sutpen as saying that he was 20 when the siege took place (310).

1827 AND AFTER

Sutpen recuperates from the wounds he suffered during the siege and becomes engaged to and marries the plantation owner's daughter.

General Compson is again the source of Sutpen's own account (317).

1832

January   Charles Bon is born.

This date comes from his headstone that Judith Sutpen had made (239). We've already heard Schoenberg question its authenticity, but the date seems consistent with other dates.

January or
after   Sutpen discovers that his first wife cannot be incorporated into his design because she is partly black.

The best evidence that Sutpen made this discovery comes from Sutpen himself through the third-person narrator (443). General Compson reports Sutpen's saying that he learned this "fact . . . after my son was born" (329). Shreve implies that this discovery occurred in 1831 (331), and Quentin seems to agree. Still, the 1832 date has, I believe, the stronger evidence: the headstone.

1833

June	Sutpen first appears in Jefferson.	The third-person narrator gives this date twice (9 and 34).

1830s–50s

Charles Bon's mother prepares him to carry out her vengeance against Sutpen.	Shreve suggests this to Quentin, who neither agrees nor disagrees (369–75). No evidence corroborates Shreve's notion that this happened although the third-person narrator judges some of Shreve's inferences about Bon's mother as "probably right" (418–20). Whether Bon is his mother's instrument or his own man, his appearance at Sutpen's Hundred has the same effect.

1835

	Clytie is born.	In 1909 Rosa says that Clytie is 74 (169).
Summer	Sutpen's French architect attempts to escape by fleeing into the river bottom. Sutpen invites General Compson and others to join in the hunt. Beside the campfire General Compson hears Sutpen's account of his early life.	Quentin tells Shreve that these events occurred "in the second summer" (272)—that is, Sutpen's second summer in Jefferson.

1838

June	Sutpen and Ellen Coldfield marry.	Rosa says that Ellen married after having "had but five" years to observe him (17), and Mr. Compson begins his description of the wedding with "It was in June of 1838, almost five years to the day from that Sunday morning when he rode into town" (56).

1839

Henry Sutpen is born.

Henry is two years older than Judith, whose gravestone dates her birth in 1841.

1840s–50s

The lawyer for Sutpen's first wife plots ways to milk the most from her, from Bon, and from Sutpen.

This, too, is Shreve's conjecture (375 ff.) unsupported by but not inconsistent with the testimony of others.

1841

October 3   Judith Sutpen is born.

The date comes from Rosa's inscription on Judith's gravestone (264).

1845

Rosa is born.

According to Rosa, she is four years younger than Judith (21) and was 19 when Bon died in May, 1865 (167). Floyd Watkins finds inconsistencies in "the difference between the ages of Rosa and Judith."[6] The differences, though, are not necessarily inconsistent. Judith's tombstone gives her birthdate as October 3, 1841. Rosa says that she is four years younger than Judith. If we suppose her to have been born in June 1845, the differences that trouble Watkins would all fit together. Rosa would have been nineteen in May 1865, as she says she was. And anytime between June and October of 1847 she would have been 3 while Judith was 6, as in the passages (23 and 26) that Watkins cites. The final passage

6. Floyd Watkins, "What Happens," 84.

that Watkins finds incon-
sistent says that Rosa was
"just four" when she vis-
ited Sutpen's Hundred. But
the weather was "hot" (27),
a fact consistent with a
birthday in the summer.

1847

Judith makes her driver let the carriage horses race.	Rosa says that Judith was 6 when she "instigated and authorised that negro to make the team run away" (26).

1849

Rosa and Mr. Coldfield visit Ellen at Sutpen's Hundred. Judith is ailing.	Rosa says that she was "just four" then (27).

1849–55

During this time Rosa and Mr. Coldfield see little of the Sutpens. Rosa's aunt, who had been keeping the Coldfields' house, leaves with a horse trader.	Rosa tells this to Quentin (29). Later, however, she seems to give a different date. (See the entry for the summer of 1860.)
On an evening during this time Judith and Henry slip into the barn loft to see one of the rough-and-tumble fights between Sutpen and his slaves. Henry screams and vomits, but Judith watches unmoved.	Rosa tells Quentin this, too (30–33).

1853

Milly Jones is born.	She was 8 when Sutpen rode off to war, according to the third-person narrator's record of Quentin's thoughts (231).

1854

Sutpen gives Wash Jones permission to squat in an abandoned fishing camp at Sutpen's Hundred.

This occurred when Milly was 1, again according to the third-person narrator's record of Quentin's thoughts (229).

1859

Charles Etienne Saint-Valery Bon is born, the son of Charles Bon and his New Orleans mistress or wife.

Charles Etienne's gravestone shows this date. Judith had given it to General Compson when she handed him the money with which to buy the gravestone and have it inscribed (239).

Fall

Henry meets Bon at the university. They spend two weeks at Sutpen's Hundred during Christmas vacation.

Mr. Compson speaks of Bon's spending two Christmases in a row at the Sutpens' plantation. Mr. Compson calls this one "that first Christmas" (125) and dates the second as December 1860 (130).

1860

Spring and summer

Henry and Bon are studying law together at the university (126). Sutpen travels to New Orleans to investigate Bon in June (113 and 127) while Henry and Bon are staying at Sutpen's Hundred (127). Bon then spends the summer in New Orleans; Henry, at home.

Mr. Compson tells Quentin all this.

Summer

Mr. Coldfield and Sutpen are both away. Rosa spends the summer with her sister Ellen at Sutpen's Hundred.

She says that she stayed there "the summer after that first Christmas that Henry brought [Bon] home, the summer following the two days of that June vacation which he spent at Sutpen's Hundred before he rode on to the

River to take the steamboat home, that summer after my aunt left and papa had to go away on business" (181). Here Rosa implies that her aunt had left with the horse trader more recently than the passage on page 29 indicates. One could argue that the words "after my aunt left" don't necessarily mean that the aunt had left in the year just before that summer. But that interpretation would violate the parallel structures that she has set up to modify "summer" wherever else it appears. So I call this a slip of Faulkner's.

Fall	Henry and Bon return to the university.	Mr. Compson reports this (130). Shreve sets the date as September, and Quentin does not dispute it (406).
Christmas Eve	Sutpen tells Henry something about Bon—presumably either that he has an octoroon mistress and a son or that he has a wife and a son in New Orleans. Henry gives his father the lie and goes to New Orleans with Bon.	Mr. Compson tells Quentin this (129–31).

1861

Spring	The Civil War having started, Henry and Bon return to the university to enlist in a company forming there.	Mr. Compson says, "That spring they returned north, into Mississippi. Bull Run had been fought" (147). The battle of Bull Run took place July 21, 1861. Henry and Bon thus would have enlisted in the spring of 1862. If we accept that date, then Henry and Bon would have lingered in New Orleans for more than a year. In writing that

Bull Run had been fought, Faulkner seems to have erred; for the war was beginning in the spring of 1861, companies were forming then, and he has the university company fight at Pittsburg Landing (Shiloh) in a battle that occurred in April 1862 (154). If Henry and Bon enlisted in 1861, then they would have spent only the months since Christmas in New Orleans, plenty of time for Henry to have seen and perhaps come to accept Bon's relationship with the octoroon.

Colonel Sartoris raises a regiment in Jefferson. Sutpen is second in command when it leaves Jefferson.	Mr. Compson tells Quentin this (97).

1862

April 6 and 7	Henry and Bon fight at Pittsburg Landing.	Mr. Compson tells Quentin this (154).

1863

January 23	Ellen Coldfield Sutpen dies.	The gravestone that Sutpen had carved gives this date (236).

1864

Mr. Coldfield dies, having nailed himself up in his attic and starved to death. Rosa moves to Sutpen's Hundred.	Mr. Compson tells Quentin this (70 and 156).
Sutpen discusses his design with General Compson in his office. Sutpen speaks of the failure of his design (341–42) even though Henry has not yet slain Bon and fled.	Talking with Shreve, Quentin says, "Sutpen came home in '64 with the two tombstones and talked to Grandfather in the office that day before both of them went back to the war" (337).

1865

March	Sutpen's unit is sent to reinforce Henry's and Bon's. Sutpen meets Bon twice but offers him no sign of recognition.	This information comes from the third-person narrator (435).
March	Shortly after those meetings, Sutpen calls for Henry. When they meet in Sutpen's tent, Sutpen tells Henry that Bon's mother "was part negro" (443).	This, too, comes from the third-person narrator (437 and 439–43).
May 3	Henry slays Bon and flees.	The date comes from the gravestone that Judith had made (239).
	Rosa moves to Sutpen's Hundred.	Watkins says that this date is in dispute. He notes that Rosa says that she stayed at the Sutpens' after going there when Charles was killed. In a passage that Watkins does not cite, she confirms that date by saying that, after staying with Ellen in the summer of 1860, "I went back home and stayed five years, heard an echoed shot, ran up a nightmare flight of stairs" (185). Even though Watkins quotes the passage on page 106 saying that Rosa "didn't go out there at once," he finds the 1865 date inconsistent with page 70, which says, "After Mr Coldfield died in '64, Miss Rosa moved out to Sutpen's Hundred." Now '65 did come after '64, but Watkins thinks the passage means that Rosa moved "soon after her father died."[7] Watkins appears to think that '65 wasn't soon enough. The "soon," how-

7. Floyd Watkins, "What Happens," 81.

ever, is his own creation.
The next four words on
page 70—"She was twenty
then"—again confirm
1865. Later in the article
Watkins confronts those
words and gets into a
deeper muddle. Because he
doesn't question his own
assumption that she moved
in 1864, he writes: "If the
year of her birth is correct,
she was at most only nineteen in 1864. . . . Why
should both Mr. Compson
and Faulkner be so aware
of age and years and yet
lapse immediately into
egregious error? Is this
subtle characterization, a
point to plant doubts about
Mr. Compson's narration,
or some sort of slip by the
author?[8] The answer is
"none of the above but a
slip of the critic's."

1866

January	After the war Sutpen returns to his plantation.	His return is described by Mr. Compson (73) and by Rosa (197).
March	Sutpen confronts and faces down the local men who want to recruit him to oppose carpetbaggers. Sutpen urges the men to follow him by restoring their land and allowing the South to save itself.	Rosa tells Quentin this (201–2).
April	Rosa and Sutpen are engaged.	Rosa tells Quentin that it "took me just three months" (197).
April	Sutpen suggests to Rosa that they should breed, but marry only if she has a boy. Rosa, out-	Rosa tells Quentin that the idea of marrying only if their child is a boy "must have been in [Sutpen's]

8. Floyd Watkins, "What Happens," 82.

raged, rejects Sutpen and moves back to her house in Jefferson.

mind for a day, a week, even a month maybe" (214). His proposition brought her life to an end, she says in 1909, "on an afternoon in April forty-three years ago' (17). Quentin obviously passed that date as well as the rest of the scene along to Shreve, who refers to the proposition as "this unbidden April's compounded demonry" (222).

1868

Wash challenges Sutpen about his attention to Milly. Sutpen implies that he will, in Wash's words, "make hit right" (355). Since this is a year before the birth of Milly's child (355), she isn't pregnant yet.

Quentin learned this from General Compson and told it to Shreve (354).

1869

August 12   Milly's and Sutpen's daughter is born. Sutpen rejects Milly and the baby. Wash kills Sutpen with a scythe, waits while the corpse is discovered and reported and while a posse gathers, cuts Milly's throat and the baby's, picks up the scythe, charges the posse, and is shot and killed.

In telling Shreve this, Quentin often attributes it with the tags "Grandfather said" and "Father said" (354–63).

1870

Summer   Charles Etienne and his mother visit Bon's grave.

Mr. Compson tells Quentin, "There was one afternoon in the summer of '70 when one of these graves . . . was actually watered by tears. Your grandfather saw it" (241).

1871

December   Clytie goes to New Orleans and brings Charles Etienne back to live at Sutpen's Hundred.

General Compson is the original source of this information. Mr. Compson says at first that Clytie might have waited until the octoroon had died and left Charles Etienne an orphan (245) but later tells Quentin, "Your grandfather said you [that is, *one*] did not wonder what had become of the mother, you did not even care: death or elopement or marriage" (245).

1879

Charles Etienne starts a brawl at a dance in the black community and seriously injures a black man. Charles Etienne is indicted and tried as a white man. While the judge is rebuking him, General Compson interrupts; and everyone suddenly realizes that Charles Etienne is partly black. General Compson gets the indictment quashed, pays the fine, and offers him money so that he can move away and pass as white. Charles Etienne leaves Jefferson.

General Compson told Mr. Compson this, and he passed it along to Quentin (252).

1880

Charles Etienne returns to Jefferson with his black wife.

Again from General Compson (257).

1881

Jim Bond is born to Charles Etienne and his wife.

General Compson once more (257).

1884

| February 12 | Judith Sutpen dies of yellow fever contracted while caring for Charles Etienne. | Rosa's inscription on Judith's gravestone gives this date (264). |
| | Charles Etienne dies of yellow fever soon after Judith's death. | Before her death Judith had given Clytie all of the inscription for Charles Etienne's gravestone (except, of course, his date of death). Clytie had saved her money and given it to General Compson to buy the stone. He had ordered it and its full inscription (239 and 263). |

1889

| | Quentin Compson is born. | When Rosa asks Quentin to meet her in her father's office, the third-person narrator dates the meeting as September 1909 and speaks of Quentin's "twenty years' heritage of breathing the same air" that Sutpen had breathed in Jefferson (9). |

About 1905

| | Henry returns to Sutpen's Hundred to die. Clytie takes care of him and keeps his presence a secret. | Shreve says that Clytie kept Henry hidden "for almost four years." Quentin does not disagree but, according to the third-person narrator, isn't listening (438). Shreve's date seems reasonable nonetheless. |

1909

| September | Before noon on a day in September, Quentin receives Rosa's note asking him to call on her. He meets with her from "two oclock until almost sundown." | The third-person narrator records this (7 and 3). |

September	During the early eve-ning of the same day Quentin talks with his father. Quentin has promised to return to Rosa's with his buggy.	The third-person narrator records this (10).
September	Later that night Quentin drives Rosa to Sutpen's Hundred. Clytie has ap-peared and lighted a lamp and is trying to keep Rosa from going upstairs. Rosa knocks her down and goes up. Quentin helps Clytie sit up, follows Rosa, and meets her hurrying back down. Quentin goes to the bedroom where he talks to Henry. Then Quentin takes Rosa home.	The third-person narrator records this (451–65).
December	Rosa sends an ambu-lance to take Henry to town. Clytie sets the house on fire and burns him and herself to death. Jim Bond is left without family or home.	Shreve dates these events (465), but they are told mainly by the third-person narrator.

1910

| January 8 | Rosa Coldfield dies. | Mr. Compson gives this date in his letter to Quen-tin (217). |
| January or February | Mr. Compson's letter leads Quentin and Shreve to discuss the Sutpens' lives in their room at Harvard. | According to the third-person narrator, the letter carried into the Harvard room "five months later" the aromas of the Septem-ber evening when Quentin and his father had discussed the Sutpens (34). Five months would place the discussion in February, a date that is entirely pos-sible. But the discussion sounds as if the letter, |

dated January 8, may have
just reached Quentin. The
"five months" probably
signifies nothing more than
Faulkner's miscounting.

Once I had laid out the fabula, what I found surprised me. It is, in the first place, longer than I had expected. That is, one can find the dates of a considerable number of events—nearly as many, I expect, as in *The Sound and the Fury* and far more than in any of the novels in the Snopes trilogy.

Next, the fabula seems to contradict what is nearly a truism among readers who write about *Absalom*. Many have seen it as Vickery does: as a "kaleidoscope" that sustains its ambiguity to the end. Yet the fabula shows that the chronology of *Absalom* is almost, though not entirely, consistent. Some readers have exaggerated the importance of inconsistencies. Watkins, for instance, contends that *Absalom* shows "that the search for fact and the speculation about meaning can never arrive at the truth." Because his argument demands inconsistencies, he went prospecting for them but too seldom assayed the nuggets he found. A few were true gold, mainly the editorial slips that Langford would later explain. Most of the other inconsistencies that Watkins found are trivial: they contribute nothing toward answering what Watkins himself sees as the book's "basic question": Why did Henry kill Charles? Far too often Watkins presents as inconsistencies his own misreadings. He attributes to Quentin an observation of the third-person narrator. He claims that Shreve "says that it was sixty years between the last days of the Civil War . . . and . . . 1909."[9] The narrator is again the speaker, and the sixty years actually go back to the Christmas in 1860 when Henry gives his father the lie—that is, roughly fifty-nine years and nine months. In analyzing the fabula, I've already touched on three other similar points where Watkins went astray. For a book with such intricate narration *Absalom* resists quite effectively the prying of those seeking to uncover inconsistency.

Many readers, too, have viewed Quentin's and Shreve's imaginings as crucial to whatever narrative coherence the book finally achieves. Waggoner expresses that position with force:

---

9. Vickery, 84–85; Floyd Watkins, "What Happens," 87, 80, 84, 86.

Absalom has many voices but no official, sanctioned Voice. . . . There is only Quentin, who speaks with no special authority, mostly in the words of others, and who does not act at all; and Shreve, who speaks as one amazed, even outraged, by a tale hard to credit and almost impossible to understand, and who, when he is not repeating what Quentin has told him, invents a version based on no uniquely privileged knowledge of the facts. Quentin and Shreve together finally imagine a version of Sutpen's story that has both plausibility and meaning, but the plausibility rests upon our willingness to accept as correct certain speculations of theirs for which they can offer no solid proof, and the meaning is left implicit.[10]

Before analyzing the narration and the fabula, I would have agreed by and large with Waggoner. Analysis, however, reveals something very like an official Voice, that of the third-person narrator. Some events in the fabula—particularly the crucial March 1865 scene in which Sutpen tells Henry that Bon's mother "was part negro"—come only from that voice. Waggoner overlooks the importance of Rosa and Mr. Compson as narrators and the importance of the gravestones as evidence. The fabula also shows that few events rise solely out of the boys' imaginings. Quentin virtually always speaks with what I would call special authority: when he's not telling about events that he himself has experienced, he draws on reports from his father and General Compson, who were usually reporting on what they had witnessed. We hear Sutpen's own voice speaking through them. The fabula lists only two entries that Shreve contributed on his own, the entries labeled "1830s-50s" and "1840s-50s." Neither is important to the course of the book. All in all, the boys' account of what happened is not speculative. The proof they offer and their plausible inferences make their account convincing, and the third-person narrator confirms it. That the meaning remains implicit would be unusual only if *Absalom* were an allegory or a fable. Finally, the fabula urges us not to heed too readily warnings like this one from Matthews: "We may finally never be able to judge what is fact and what fiction in the mutual tellings, as threatens to become an end-

10. Waggoner, 148–49.

less critical amusement."[11] While we may never be able to mark every event "fact" or "fiction," our ability to mark so many encourages us to consider the book as one story, not as a collection of only somewhat coherent accounts.

11. Matthews, 120.

3
The Characters' Designs

ALTHOUGH SOME NARRATIVE TECHNIQUES still call for investigation, we know enough about the reliability of the six narrators and about the fabula to pursue once more the designs of characters. Those other than Sutpen have, of course, their own plans and perhaps schemes; and all those designs bear upon Sutpen's and ultimately suffice to thwart it.

Ellen, Rosa, and Milly share a design: to marry Sutpen. What makes that goal so enticing? Mr. Compson attributes to Rosa the most general, and cynical, answer as he describes Ellen's aunt's motives for sanctioning Ellen's marriage to Sutpen. She may have married "for the sake of that big house and the position and state which the women realised long before the men did that he not only aimed at but was going to attain. Or maybe women are even less complex than that and to them any wedding is better than no wedding" (61). Both of those motives—to gain position and to avoid spinsterhood—may have driven all three women and may suffice to explain why Ellen married Sutpen. Those motives recur when Mr. Compson recalls how Rosa had described the way Ellen had spoken of Judith's marrying Bon:

> Ellen did not once mention love between Judith and Bon. She did not hint around it. Love, with reference to them,

was just a finished and perfectly dead subject like the matter of virginity would be after the birth of the first grand-
child. She spoke of Bon as if he were three inanimate
objects in one or perhaps one inanimate object for which
she and her family would find three concordant uses: a gar-
ment which Judith might wear as she would a riding habit
or a ball gown, a piece of furniture which would com-
plement and complete the furnishing of her house and
position, and a mentor and example to correct Henry's
provincial manners and speech and clothing. (90–91).

If love had ever entered into Ellen's conception of Judith's marriage, it did so only initially. Later, certainly, Ellen dismissed it
and moved to what she found important: status. The daughter of
a high-minded, barely solvent county-store owner adopted the
standards of the aristocracy or, at least, the would-be aristocracy.
She may have thus made Sutpen as much her instrument as she
was his.

Rosa has two designs, and both fail. Her first design she
forms when Ellen, dying, begs, "Protect her, at least. At least save
Judith" (22). Rosa the romantic turns that plea into her quest. She
hopes to shield the innocent maiden Judith from the devices of her
father the ogre; and so when Wash brings word that Henry has
killed Bon, Rosa rushes to Judith's aid. At the staircase Clytie bars
her way. Rosa, fearing that she will arrive too late, is struggling to
pass when Judith calls down from the stairhead—to Clytie. Judith
seeks no aid from Rosa, who finds her quest misbegotten. Rosa
tells Quentin, "I had come, not too late as I had thought, but
come too soon"(168). She must wait a while to form her next
design, her engagement to Sutpen.

Rosa engages herself to Sutpen for motives more complicated than Ellen's. Talking to Quentin in 1909, she eliminates
many of the motives that one might imagine for her engagement.
She does not plead ignorance. Ellen, she said, had had only a little
time and opportunity to see what Sutpen was; Rosa herself "had
had twenty years in which to watch him" (17). Rosa also admits
that Ellen's example might have warned her away. "I saw what
had happened to Ellen, my sister. . . . I saw the price which she
had paid for that house and that pride" (17). Nor does she "plead
youth" or "propinquity" or "material necessity" although she de-
fies anyone to blame her for "accepting the honorable proffer of

marriage from the man whose food she was forced to subsist on"
(18). Nor will she plead that she was attracted to Sutpen because
he was a military hero (19). Only many pages later does she begin
to explain her motives. As Linda Kauffman has shown, Rosa's narrative is not the raving of a madwoman but a lover's discourse:
"Outrage is a major characteristic of lovers' discourses from Ar-
iadne's lament to Theseus to *The Letters of a Portuguese Nun*.
Whenever the lover is abandoned, in fact, the tone of the discourse
is frequently furious, characteristically wavering between hope
and despair, fury and fortitude. These are precisely the polarities
that shape Rosa's narrative. . . . Rosa herself is both an enemy and
a lover. The object of her worship is Charles Bon; the object of
both her desire and her enmity is Thomas Sutpen."[1] The term
lover ordinarily implies more than Kauffman intends: after all, Ar-
iadne and the nun consummated their loves. But the term, nar-
rowed as Kauffman uses it, fits Rosa's narrative. Kauffman is right
in saying that Rosa worshipped Bon and desired and hated
Sutpen.

Rosa describes quite clearly her feelings toward Sutpen. With
Judith and Clytie, Rosa waited at Sutpen's Hundred for Sutpen to
return. They all waited for the same reason: "Not that we would
or did need him" but "knowing that he would need us" because
he would "return a sonless widower, barren of that posterity
which he doubtless must have wanted who had gone to the
trouble and expense of getting children and housing them among
imported furniture beneath crystal chandeliers" (192–93). All
three women, Rosa says, expect Sutpen to start again "the Her-
culean task . . . into which . . . he would undoubtedly sweep us
with the old ruthlessness whether we would or no" (196). And
Rosa would—she is waiting for him to sweep her into his design,
even though she doesn't know what it is. As he describes his plans
for what remains of Sutpen's Hundred, she thinks that he speaks
like madman and a child. Even so, she says to herself, "At last my
life is worth something, even though it only shields and guards
the antic fury of an insane child" (202). When shortly thereafter
he announces that he will marry her, she lets her silence mean
consent. His needing her gives her life meaning.

When Sutpen sends Judith for her mother's wedding ring and
puts it on Rosa's finger, Rosa understands that for him she simply

---

1. Kauffman, "Devious Channels," 188.

replaces Ellen in his design "as though in the restoration of that ring to a living finger he had turned all time back twenty years and stopped it." His single-mindedness strikes her as an impetuous madness; nevertheless, she will surrender herself to it. "I . . . told myself, 'Why, he is mad. He will decree this marriage for tonight and perform his own ceremony, himself both groom and minister; pronounce his own wild benediction on it with the very bedward candle in his hand: and I mad too, for I will acquiesce, succumb; abet him and plunge down'" (206).If he had asked, her "surprised importunate traitorous flesh" would have made her give herself to him that night (206). She was imagining him a man lost in a dark swamp and herself as the sun that guides him to solid ground and air and light (207–8). She could then have said to him, "O furious mad old man, I hold no substance that will fit your dream but I can give you airy space and scope for your delirium" (209–10).

He doesn't ask though. Days go by while he struggles to save whatever he can of Sutpen's Hundred and of his design. Slipping the ring onto Rosa's finger, however, did not stop time. Sutpen eventually sees that his time for completing his design is running out. Mr. Compson imagines him stopped dead in some furrow at the realization that "possibly he could get but one more son, had at best but one more son in his loins, as the old cannon might know when it has just one more shot in its corporeality" (348). In that instant Sutpen decides, as Shreve phrases it, to suggest to Rosa "that they breed together for test and sample and if it was a boy they would marry" (222). The notion clashes with and destroys her romantic, idealistic design of herself as his shield and guard, as his sun. Appalled, she rejects him and returns to live in Jefferson. She has then become the woman whose narrative stance we'll consider in the next chapter.

Milly, unlike Rosa, succumbs to Sutpen. She is seduced by him and by her desire to complete her own design. She can't help knowing that she's doing wrong. Her father questions her; her own behavior attests to her feelings of guilt. When she wears Sutpen's gifts, she is "not quite defiant and not quite cringing and not quite flaunting the ribbons and the beads, but almost; not quite any of them but a little of all: bold sullen and fearful" (353). She must, of course, have been seduced by Sutpen's wealth, even though it's much diminished; by his social prominence; and by his military fame. In that she resembles Ellen. But Wash's admiration for Sutpen must sway her too. And so must Wash's confidence in Sutpen, confidence that Wash expresses—movingly, I think—when he says to Sutpen, "I know that whatever your hands tech, whether hit's a regiment of men or a ignorant gal or just a hound dog, that you will make hit right" (355). So, almost as if she had accepted the suggestion that Rosa refused, Milly bears Sutpen's child. If it had been a boy, her design would have been fulfilled: she would have supplanted Rosa in Ellen's house as well as her bed (166). But it is a girl, and as a consequence Milly is rejected by Sutpen and slain by her father.

The design "to marry Sutpen" thus shapes much of the life of three of the book's characters. Mr. Compson compares Ellen to the caterpillar that breaks out of its cocoon, blossoms into a butterfly, gets tossed around in a gale, weakens, and dies. She married Sutpen, bloomed "into a perennial bright vacuum of arrested sun" (84), turned into a "bright trivial shell" (103), and died. In marrying Sutpen and completing her design, she had made her life wither away. The completion of her design, however, had advanced Sutpen toward success with his own design. Next, Rosa's design calls for her to shield Sutpen while he engages in activities that she sees as pointless and that are in fact unsuccessful; but her design fails when his pragmatism violates her propriety. The failure of her design leaves her frozen in an attitude of rejection for her last forty-three years. And finally the failure of Milly's design leaves her dead, makes Sutpen see that his design has also failed, and leads directly to Sutpen's own death. All these women's designs intertwine with his, their successes and failures mirroring his.

All of Sutpen's children strive to be as dauntless as he is. That design isn't easy to achieve. While watching Sutpen and his slave in their catch-as-catch-can struggle in the stable, Henry reveals a weakness by plunging, "screaming and vomiting" (31), out of the crowd and into his mother's arms. Two of Sutpen's other children, Judith and Clytie, watch unmoved. But once Henry has decided to foster a marriage between Bon and Judith, he drives single-mindedly ahead. He calls his father a liar, leaves his heritage behind, overlooks the octoroon's existence, and blinks at incest. Sutpen can turn Henry against the marriage only by telling him that Bon is black. Henry then bars the marriage as vigorously as he had sought it

Bon pursues his designs with equal resolution. Determined

to win from Sutpen a word or at least a gesture of acknowledgment, he befriends Henry, allows himself to become Judith's de facto fiancé, accompanies Henry throughout the war, wins his consent, and writes Judith a letter that she takes as proposing marriage. But as soon as Bon has realized that Sutpen will never acknowledge him, he changes his design: he will force Henry to kill him. That design Bon follows, unwavering, to its end and his.

Charles Etienne inherits the Sutpen propensity for designs that fail and for dauntlessness, too. Although everyone in the county regards him as white, he starts a fight "for no reason" (253). General Compson, seeing him on trial, realizes that he is black, pays his fine, and urges him to go away where he can continue passing as white. He leaves, only to return a year later with "a coal black and ape-like woman and an authentic wedding license" that he "apparently flung . . . in Judith's face with something of that invincible despair with which he had attacked the negroes in the dice game" (257). Sutpen, Bon, and Henry kept striving toward their designs with undaunted hope, giving up hope only when failure was plain. For Charles Etienne it is despair that is invincible. Apparently able to pass as black or white, whichever he wishes, he refuses to live as either. He seeks situations in which to "flaunt and fling" his black wife at anyone "who would retaliate: the negro stevedores and deckhands on steamboats or in city honky-tonks who thought he was a white man and believed it only the more strongly when he denied it; the white men who, when he said he was a negro, believed that he lied in order to save his skin, or worse: from sheer besotment of sexual perversion; in either case the result the same" (258). He strikes the first blow, fights with "fury and implacability and physical imperviousness to pain," and takes a beating, "laughing" (259). Until his death from yellow fever, he repeats this cycle, hopeless but not daunted.

Looking down from the stable loft at what outraged Ellen and made Henry vomit, the two girls watched undaunted. Since I'll soon discuss Clytie as a Sutpen and can touch on her dauntlessness then, let's turn to Judith, whom Mr. Compson calls "the Sutpen with the ruthless Sutpen code of taking what it wanted provided it were strong enough, of the two children as Henry was the Coldfield with the Coldfield cluttering of morality and rules of right and wrong" (149). Mr. Compson overstates his contrast. She is far from oblivious to morality, as he shows on the next page where he imagines Judith's saying to herself: "I love, I will accept no substitute; something has happened between him and my father; if my father was right, I will never see him again, if wrong he will come or send for me; if happy I can be I will, if suffer I must I can" (150). But the force of those last main verbs—in *I will* and *I can*—reveals her strength; Sutpen's return from the war puts it to the proof. As Rosa reports, the words that the father and the daughter speak are laconic: "'Well, daughter . . . Henry's not—?' 'No. He's not here.'—'Ah. And—?' 'Yes. Henry killed him'" (198). The restraint that she had exercised since Bon's death breaks for a moment: she bursts into tears. But they evaporate "as instantaneously as if the very fierce and arid aura which [Sutpen] had enclosed her in were drying the tears faster than they emerged" (199). Grief does not daunt her. If she must suffer, she can. In fact, she and Clytie face whatever comes with even more fortitude than the Sutpen men do. When designs collapse, the men despair; the women endure.

Because Henry, Bon, and Judith have inherited Sutpen's perseverance, they work toward their designs as single-mindedly as he works toward his. Henry strives to make his brother his brother-in-law; Bon, to compel his father to acknowledge him; Judith, to be happy if she can. Their designs all go counter to Sutpen's; and since his children press on undaunted, they contribute to the failure of his design.

In two words Henry describes another of the characters' designs. As he tells Quentin, Henry has come home "to die" (464). In 1865 he had destroyed the design he cherished, to bring Bon into the family as his brother-in-law. With that design forever beyond reach, Henry has left the last forty-four years of his life, so far as we know, a blank. Clytie sees to it that he—and she—complete his last design. She plans to set Sutpen's Hundred afire, and they both perish in the blaze.

Dying in the fire, Clytie brings her own design to its culmination. Shreve imagines her "tragic gnome's face" looking down at Rosa "perhaps not even now with triumph and no more of despair than it had ever worn, possibly even serene" (468). That complex of emotions stems from the outcome of her overall design. Quentin and Shreve perceive only a sliver of it. When Quentin and Rosa invade Sutpen's Hundred, Clytie indicates to Quentin that she is protecting Henry: "Whatever he done, me and Judith and him have paid it out" (461). From that, Shreve surmises that

Clytie set fire to the house to protect Henry from prosecution for Bon's murder (465–66). Shreve is right, I think, as far as he goes. If his interpretation were complete, Clytie would presumably have died with Henry because she wanted to avoid prosecution herself for arson and for his death. Rosa, however, sees more of Clytie's design than the two boys—and most critics—do.

But there are two exceptions. Loren F. Schmidtberger has argued that Clytie may have known that "Judith's suitor was their half-brother; that Henry was guilty of fratricide."[2] Schmidtberger shows how Clytie could have gained that knowledge; but since Clytie seems not to have revealed what she knows, her knowledge can bear at best only slightly on the reader's experience of *Absalom*. Thadious M. Davis has gone far toward clarifying Clytie's importance by considering her role as a black Sutpen. Davis points out that Clytie "has no private life as a black person. She is bereft of all that gave meaning to black life: the black family and the black church." She is Sutpen's daughter. In other Faulkner books mulatto daughters of their white masters are sometimes just servants, but Clytie is a Sutpen. As Davis says, "Clytie is where she belongs. There are no possibilities suggested for her living apart from Sutpen's Hundred and her blood kin."[3]

Davis emphasizes Clytie as Judith's "black twin," their relationship paralleling Bon's and Henry's. Few critics have noted that parallel, and none has worked it out so carefully as Davis has: "Their relationship is a more sustained and meaningful version of that between Henry and Charles. Because Clytie and Judith relate to each other as 'womenfolk' first, then as 'daughter' and 'sister,' they escape the burden placed on their brothers. . . . [Clytie and Judith] are locked into a narrow existence; uncomplaining and stoical, they make the best of their lives." At this point Davis and I part company, mainly because we are bound for different destinations. She highlights Clytie's family relationships that span the barriers between races and classes. Davis finds in Faulkner's portrayal of Clytie hopeful signs for a society in which people can "see themselves and accept humanity in others."[4] I'm not yet ready to look out at the world and away from the book. In fact, I want to carry Davis's argument further and to qualify it a little.

2. Schmidtberger, "*Absalom, Absalom! What Clytie Knew*," 263.

3. Thadious Davis, "Yoking," 210.

4. Ibid., 211, 211–12, 218.

Like Davis, Rosa sees Clytie as a Sutpen and even pairs her off with Judith. Rosa tells Quentin how Ellen burst into the stable where Sutpen was fighting one of his slaves. Henry ran screaming to his mother, but Ellen couldn't find Judith. Rosa imagines looking up at the loft and seeing "two Sutpen faces this time—once on Judith and once on the negro girl beside her" (33). That is the book's first mentioning of Clytie. And later Rosa describes Clytie's face as "Sutpen face enough" (169).

Nevertheless, Rosa sees in Clytie something other than Sutpen. Davis regards Clytie as utterly isolated from her black heritage: "Her mother, one of the original band of Sutpen slaves, is not even given to her as memory." However, as Davis says nine lines later, Clytie "is never shown directly; what she feels remains a mystery."[5] Since that's so, we can't know what she remembers. Yet we do have Rosa's perceptions; in fact, they're almost all we have of Clytie. Rosa sees that Clytie's face is "at once both more and less than Sutpen" (174). In Clytie, Rosa feels "a brooding awareness and acceptance of the inexplicable unseen inherited from an older and a purer race than mine" (171). Rosa is thus aware that Clytie draws much of her being from her black mother. Indeed, Rosa fixes the proportions at half and half: "half untamed black, half Sutpen blood" (195). Emancipated, Clytie is free, Rosa says, "yet incapable of freedom," not like a tamed animal unable to return to the wild, but as a person who "had never once called herself a slave." Her ancestors are the blacks whom Rosa (and Mr. Compson) called "wild." Rosa does not make that adjective a pejorative. On the contrary, as she says, "if 'untamed' be synonymous with 'wild', then 'Sutpen' is the silent unsleeping viciousness of the tamer's lash." The white Sutpen half of Clytie is oppressing the half that inherits from her black mother's older and purer race. Clytie's untamed black half, on the other hand, has never been suppressed. That half, Rosa says, still holds "fidelity to none." It resembles "the indolent and solitary wolf or bear . . . whose false seeming holds it docile to fear's hand" but who is truly faithful "only to the prime fixed principle of its own savageness" (195).

But if Clytie is only half Sutpen, why does she serve the Sutpen interests so wholeheartedly? Does the lash of the word *Sutpen* somehow drive her? The answer is plainly no. She's not

5. Ibid., 210.

driven any more than her mother and Sutpen's other slaves were driven to serve him. He does not seem to have compelled them by force or by threat. He met them man against man in the stable and perhaps man against men before that in Haiti, where he ended the siege by walking out into the darkness and subduing the insurgents,

> maybe by yelling louder, maybe by standing, bearing more than they believed any bones and flesh could or should (should, yes: that would be the terrible thing: to find flesh to stand more than flesh should be asked to stand); maybe at last they themselves turning in horror and fleeing from the white arms and legs shaped like theirs and from which blood could be made to spurt and flow as it could from theirs and containing an indomitable spirit which should have come from the same primary fire which theirs came from but which could not have, could not possibly have. (317)

The blacks from Haiti take him as their leader: "Sutpen never raised his voice at them . . . instead he led them, caught them at the psychological instant by example, by some ascendancy of forbearance rather than by brute fear" (41). They are "the only men on whom he could depend" (66) because they have allied themselves to his indomitable spirit. So has Clytie's untamed black half born from their older, purer race. And in her other half, which is Sutpen, she bears her own indomitable Sutpen spirit. Her design, therefore, is both to serve and to *be* Sutpen. Consequently, when the flames are swirling around her and she judges how she has carried out her design, she can look down "perhaps not even now with triumph and no more of despair than [her face] had ever worn, possibly even serene" (468).

Bon's designs are among the most problematic because we see him so often only at a distance. Rosa, who could of course have talked with Bon, didn't. In words that might describe the reader's plight in interpreting *Absalom,* Rosa says, "I never saw him. I never even saw him dead. I heard an echo, but not the shot; I saw a closed door but did not enter it" (187). No one else passed along his words as General Compson did Sutpen's—except for Bon's letter that Judith kept and gave to General Compson's wife, the letter that Mr. Compson hands to Quentin and Quentin reads. The letter contains none of the self-revelation that one might hope for, no outright expression of Bon's feelings, not even a clear-cut allusion to Judith's. Nowhere in the letter can one find a passage to point to and say, "There, see that. Bon loved Judith." Nor can one use the letter to prove that he didn't love her—or that she loved or didn't love him. Yet if one reads the letter carefully, as Elisabeth Muhlenfeld does in "We Have Waited Long Enough," one can infer that Bon and Judith did love one another. The letter's point, although enveloped in Bon's war-weariness and his rhetorical ornamentation and especially his irony, is plain: "We have waited long enough. . . . I do not add, expect me. Because I cannot say when to expect me. Because what WAS is one thing, and now it is not because it is dead, it died in 1861, and therefore what IS . . . is something else again because it was not even alive then. And since . . . I now believe that you and I are, strangely enough, included among those who are doomed to live" (162–63). Judith understands his words: with Clytie she makes her wedding dress. Nevertheless, his letter says nothing directly about his motives or Judith's feelings or Henry's or Sutpen's opposition. In constructing our inferences, we have to get whatever we need from people who lack firsthand knowledge—Mr. Compson, Quentin, and Shreve—and from the third-person narrator.

Mr. Compson himself is puzzled by what he knows. Even for him it doesn't add up.

> We have a few old mouth-to-mouth tales; we exhume from old trunks and boxes and drawers letters without salutation or signature, in which men and women who once lived and breathed are now merely initials or nicknames out of some now incomprehensible affection which sound to us like Sanskrit or Chocktaw; we see dimly people, the people in whose living blood and seed we ourselves lay dormant and waiting, in this shadowy attenuation of time possessing now heroic proportions, performing their acts of simple passion and simple violence, impervious to time and inexplicable—Yes, Judith, Bon, Henry, Sutpen: all of them. (124)

Although he suspects that their acts have sunk so deeply into the past that no one can now recover them, he continues to grapple for their meaning. He does not recover it all—for instance, he seems to have failed to discover for himself that Bon was partly black—and yet his inferences prove valuable. In chapter 3 he gives

Quentin sketchy accounts of how Henry met Bon at the university and brought him home, of Henry's close relationship to Judith, and of the quarrel between Henry and his father. In chapter 4 he fleshes out those accounts for Quentin and for us. He tells about how he thinks Bon prepared Henry to meet the octoroon in New Orleans, how the two young men went off to war together, and how the women at Sutpen's Hundred survived the hardships of the war. It is even Mr. Compson who speaks of Henry's bringing Bon and Judith together as "perhaps . . . the pure and perfect incest" (119), making the argument himself that critics usually assign to Quentin as a carryover from *The Sound and the Fury.* After Rosa's summons has sharpened Quentin's interest in the puzzles of the Sutpens, Mr. Compson's inferences hone it; and Shreve then joins Quentin in seeking solutions. Mr. Compson thus furthers the search.

Quentin and Shreve begin their deliberations where he left off. Despite Mr. Compson's having spoken of incest, he appears to have used the word only metaphorically to characterize Henry's feelings, not literally to describe Bon's relationship to Judith. Quentin and Shreve, however, come to see that Bon is the Sutpen children's half brother. Quentin and Shreve soon realize that Bon was not so much interested in marrying Judith as in compelling Sutpen to acknowledge him. When Bon realizes that no acknowledgment will ever come, he immediately takes the step that he knows will compel Henry to kill him. One design having failed, Bon forms another. He chooses to die, not to commit suicide but to have himself killed.

Wash, too, chooses to die by having himself killed. After slaying Sutpen in the dawn, Wash sits throughout the day in the window of his house. Having seen a boy discover the body, Wash knows that "men of Sutpen's own kind" must be forming a posse; but he has decided not to flee. Quentin gives Shreve Mr. Compson's explanation of Wash's decision. It seemed to Wash "probably that he had no less to run from than he had to run to; that if he ran he would be fleeing merely one set of bragging and evil shadows for another, since they (men) were all of a kind throughout all of earth which he knew, and he old, too old to run far even if he were to run who could never escape them, no matter how much or how far he ran" (361). Unwilling to flee, Wash will not defend himself, either in the courts or behind barricades in his house. After murdering his daughter and the baby, he leaves his "razor-sharp" (363) butcher knife, seizes the scythe, and charges at the posse. "He was running toward them all, de Spain said, running into the lanterns so that now they could see the scythe raised above his head; they could see his face, his eyes too, as he ran with the scythe above his head, straight into the lanterns and the gun barrels, making no sound, no outcry while de Spain ran backward before him, saying, 'Jones! Stop! Stop, or I'll kill you. Jones! Jones! JONES!'" (364). Wash had designed his death.

And so had Sutpen. According to the midwife, Wash had been standing outside the house when Sutpen entered; according to Mr. Compson, Wash might even have taken Sutpen's reins as he dismounted. When Sutpen demanded to know the child's sex—"horse or mare?"—and the midwife told him, he stood for a moment still and silent. Then the midwife "saw his eyes and then his teeth inside his beard" (356–57). Those are Sutpen gestures that recur in the narrative when Henry, too, realizes that a design of his has utterly failed. Just after Bon has told him that Sutpen "could have stopped me," Bon sees the same movements: "His face is working; Bon can see his teeth within the soft beard which covers his sunken cheeks, and the whites of Henry's eyes as though the eyeballs struggled in their sockets" (445). Believing that he has fired his cannon's last shot, Sutpen finally, at this instant, knows that he has failed, that he will never attain his design; and so he chooses to die.

He puts that design into effect immediately. With Wash standing on the porch, Sutpen says, "Well, Milly; too bad you're not a mare too. Then I could give you a decent stall in the stable." When Sutpen steps outside, Wash repeats the insult he has overheard. The expression on his face makes Sutpen stop. "Stand back," he says. "Dont you touch me." "I'm going to tech you, Kernel." "Stand back, Wash!" (357). Then with his riding crop Sutpen strikes Wash twice. The midwife, still inside, heard the blows; and, Quentin says, the posse "found the two welts on Wash's face that night. Maybe the two blows even knocked him down; maybe it was while he was getting up that he put his hand on the scythe" (360). From Quentin's account Shreve rightly concludes that Sutpen had taunted Wash into killing him (365). To die when one's quest fails was thus Sutpen's design and that of other characters in *Absalom*.

Other characters also follow another pattern of action like Sutpen's: they resist being turned away from the plantation door.

Bon is the obvious example. Shreve infers that Bon saw the similarity and protested to Henry that Sutpen "just told you, sent me a message like you send a command by a nigger servant to a beggar or a tramp to clear out" (426).

The less obvious example is Wash Jones. Before the war, according to Quentin, Wash "had not even been allowed to approach the front of the house" (229). During the war a "black"—Clytie—made him continue coming to the back door and even then wouldn't let him in. "Stop right where you is," she would say. "You aint never crossed this door while Colonel was here and you aint going to cross it now." Quentin, however, adds a qualifying comment: "Which was true, only Father said there was a kind of pride in it: that he had never tried to enter the house, even though he believed that if he had tried, Sutpen would not have let them repulse him; like (Father said) he might have said to himself *The reason I wont try it aint that I refuse to give any black nigger the chance to tell me I cant but because I aint going to force Mister Tom to have to cuss a nigger or take a cussing from his wife on my account"* (351). When, after the war, Sutpen and Wash would drink wine in the arbor and Sutpen would get drunk, Wash would take him home, help him upstairs and into bed, and lie on the floor beside him till dawn. All that may confirm Wash's belief that, if he had sought admission, Sutpen wouldn't have turned him away. Yet in the end, after Wash has heard Sutpen insult and abandon Milly and has slain him, Wash still feels utterly rejected and despairs for himself and for his granddaughter and her baby: "Better if his kind and mine too had never drawn the breath of life on this earth. Better that all who remain of us be blasted from the face of it than that another Wash Jones should see his whole life shredded from him and shrivel away like a dried shuck thrown onto the fire" (362–63). The last figure of speech in his brief interior monologue expresses clearly and poignantly what Sutpen the boy felt but could not express as he retreated from the plantation door into the woods.

The final design that characters often repeat is, ironically, that of opening the door to the stranger. Henry wants to take Bon in even before Henry realizes that they are half brothers. Henry says: " 'If I had a brother, I wouldn't want him to be a younger brother' and [Bon]: 'Ah?' and the youth: 'No. I would want him to be older than me' and he: 'No son of a landed father wants an older brother' and the youth: 'Yes. I do. . . . Yes. And I would want him to be just like you'" (394–95). Only when Henry finally comes to know exactly who Bon is does Henry shut Bon out. In opening the door, Henry was a Sutpen; but he closed it as a Coldfield, "with the Coldfield cluttering of morality and rules of right and wrong" (149).

Judith and Clytie, the true Sutpens, hold the door open to Charles Etienne, a little boy who comes mighty close to being the kind of "nameless stranger" Sutpen was waiting for. Mr. Compson tells Quentin that in December 1871 Clytie went to New Orleans and brought him back, an orphan. General Compson never knew, according to Mr. Compson, whether taking Charles Etienne in was Judith's idea or Clytie's (245); whichever it was, they tried to make it possible for him "to shut that door himself forever behind him on all that he had ever known" (326).

Their design resembles Sutpen's: both designs were meant to go against societal patterns. Racist patterns treated people with as little as a sixty-fourth black ancestry as black and barred the creation of families made up of whites and "blacks." Judith and Clytie, the white and the "black" half sisters, want to find a way to take into their household the "black" orphan of Judith's "black" fiancé and their "black" half brother. Southern culture had no patterns permitting such an act and had strong patterns—"miscegenation" and "incest" among them—condemning it. Judith and Clytie fail to find a way through the thickets of society's prejudices and their own, and so their design turns out badly. As we've already seen, their upbringing leaves Charles Etienne an unhappy, self-lacerating man.

In an interior monologue Quentin thinks about Charles Etienne's return to Sutpen's Hundred with his black wife. Quentin wonders "what moral restoration [Judith] might have contemplated in the privacy of that house." Knowing that Charles Etienne continued living on the plantation until his death, Quentin infers that Judith must have ruthlessly compelled her own beliefs through a series of transformations. He imagines her saying to Charles Etienne: "I believed that there were things which still mattered just because they had mattered once. But I was wrong. Nothing matters but breath, breathing, to know and to be alive." Not knowing of her father's first marriage, she suggests what we see as an ironic solution: that Charles Etienne set his wife aside because she is black. Judith proposes that the wife remain at Sutpen's Hundred and starts to add that Clytie can bring up the child to whom the wife will soon give birth. But then Judith reconsiders: "No: I. I will. I will raise it" (260). She is leading up to a plan for Charles Etienne to pass as white: "We will have General Compson sell some of the land . . . and you can go. Into the North, the cities, where it will not matter even if—But they will not. They will not dare. I will tell them that you are Henry's son and who could or would dare to dispute." Charles Etienne listens without expression. She appeals to him by murmuring his name: "Charles." At last he answers, "No, Miss Sutpen." He has refused to leave; he has chosen to stay. And when he has done so, she takes the step that Sutpen felt he could not take. By saying, "Call me Aunt Judith, Charles," she opens the door (261).

Set against what Sutpen and Henry have done, her act is deeply ironic. She didn't find it effortless; her altering her plans for Charles Etienne reveals her struggling to discover what to do. Yet she had already realized that "nothing matters but breath, breathing, to know and to be alive," a realization that the men never achieve. As we hear her say, "Call me Aunt Judith" to the "black" man who is her distant relation, her half nephew, we see in the background the two men standing silent, Sutpen unable to say to his "black" son, "Call me Father," and Henry, who can accept incest, still unable to say to a "black," "Call me your wife's brother." The tension between their designs and the things that they believed "still mattered just because they had mattered once" has paralyzed them. While they stand frozen, unable to speak the words that would open the door, Judith says simply, "Call me Aunt Judith," takes the nameless stranger into the family, and, without knowing about Sutpen's design, comes nearer to completing it than he ever does.

The irony, however, is double. Although Sutpen imagined that opening the door would save the nameless stranger, the open door does little to improve Charles Etienne's plight. He has a place to live and has care when he needs it. Nonetheless, as Mr. Compson says, Charles Etienne keeps walking down "the thorny and flint-paved path toward the Gethsemane which he had decreed and created for himself, where he had crucified himself and come down from his cross for a moment and now returned to it" (261–62). He enjoys his cross; and his suffering, unlike Christ's, redeems no one.

Indeed, the irony is triple. Sutpen told General Compson

that the nameless stranger, once admitted, would be able to look down the years at his descendants who would never even have "to know that they had once been riven forever free from brutehood" (326). Charles Etienne probably can't see far into the future: he dies when his son is about three. But we, who see further, leave that son, "Jim Bond, the scion, the last of his race" (468), howling alone in the dark woods and sunk irretrievably in brutehood. The characters' designs—to marry, to be dauntless, to die, not to be turned away, and to open the door—have culminated, like a collision of particles of matter and anti-matter, in a tremendous release of energy and in a mutual cancellation.

4

The Narrators' Designs

BY CONSIDERING IN CHAPTER 2 how the narrators acquired information, evaluated it, and made inferences from it, I treated the narration as if it were a historical account whose reliability we were trying to judge. That chapter went no further than the admittedly arbitrary line between such "factual" matters and the ways the narrators color their accounts. But now—with Sutpen's design, the basics of the narration, the fabula, and the other characters' designs in hand—we are ready to cross that line to ask a new question: What kinds of stories do the narrators believe themselves to be creating?

Not a single one of the narrators answers that question directly, and yet all of them indicate the ways they conceive of the story, the ways in which they make their narratives "fit the preconceived" (395). The answers we work out will illuminate the differing emphases that must inevitably come if, for example, one narrator considers the story a tragedy and another narrator considers it a quest-romance. The answers will round off the analysis of the narrative. But they will also look ahead to the next chapter, which takes up the designs that readers have found in *Absalom*.

Let's start with Rosa's narrative, not because hers is the first voice we hear—in fact, we hear the third-person narrator and then a dozen lines of Quentin's interior monologue before Rosa speaks—but because her voice and her vision are so forceful. That force comes from her fixation on Sutpen, a fixation that many readers say began with his proposition that they have a child and marry if it were a boy. To be sure, the insult she felt has stayed fresh; she still recalls it, literally calls it back, when, as the narrator says, her voice evokes Sutpen "by outraged recapitulation" (4). But while the view of those readers isn't false, it doesn't explain why Rosa tells the story to Quentin. She herself tries to mislead him about her motive by saying that she is telling him about Sutpen because someday Quentin may "enter the literary profession. . . . You will be married then I expect and perhaps your wife will want a new gown . . . and you can write this and submit it to the magazines." Although he says, "Yessum," he doesn't believe her but thinks, "Only she dont mean that" (6–7). Nevertheless, he still fails to grasp her motive and imagines "it's because she wants it told . . . so that people . . . will read it and know at last why God let us lose the War: that only through the blood of our men and the tears of our women could He stay this demon and efface his name and lineage from the earth." But he promptly dismisses that notion, too, because he realizes that Rosa is, after all, a writer herself: "If she had merely wanted it told, written and even printed, she would not have needed to call in anybody" (8). Quentin can't discover her motive; Mr. Compson has to reveal it to him—"It's because she will need someone to go with her—a man, a gentleman, yet one still young enough to do what she wants" (10). Rosa's melodramatic narrative does no doubt fit her own frame of mind, but her narrative is more than mere self-expression. As a writer and, more exactly, as an oral storyteller she narrates the story so that it will fascinate and persuade her audience. That is, she uses the story to get Quentin to accompany her to Sutpen's Hundred.

The word *melodramatic* has so far served as a tag for the kind of story Rosa tells. Yet if we attend to what she says, the tag soon proves imprecise for describing the mélange of subgenres she alludes to. Even before Rosa begins to speak, the narrator, describing how she evokes Sutpen, introduces the Gothic machinery that I've italicized here: "The *ghost* mused with *shadowy* docility as if it were the voice which he *haunted* where a more fortunate one would have had a house. Out of quiet *thunderclap* he would *abrupt* (*man-horse-demon*) upon a scene peaceful and decorous as a school-prize water color, faint *sulphur-reek* still in hair clothes and beard"

(4). By piling up such images, the passage stresses the Gothic and emphasizes it still more by introducing it so early in the book. Yet even here we should notice that the passage twice undercuts the Gothic by plunking its "hero" into comically inappropriate settings: the unlucky ghost reduced to haunting a voice, the Heathcliff who manifests himself upon . . . what? A moor? A mountaintop? No, a nice little painting by a schoolchild.

Nevertheless, the Gothic elements keep cropping up. While their first appearance warns us against taking them too seriously, we can never dismiss them either. But we must mesh them with other subgenres that also inform Rosa's narrative. Sometimes she considers the story tragic. Sutpen's finding Ellen in a church makes Rosa suspect a "fatality and curse on the South and on our family" (20). Sutpen himself might be "brute instrument of that justice which presides over human events which, incept in the individual, runs smooth, less claw than velvet: but which, by man or woman flouted, drives on like fiery steel and overrides both weakly just and unjust strong" (166–67). More often she regards the story as a fairy tale. In the garden where Bon walked with Judith, Rosa felt a "fairy-tale to come alive" (182). From her aunt, Mr. Compson says, Rosa had learned to think of Ellen's marriage as taking her "into an edifice like Bluebeard's" (71). Time after time Rosa calls the story an ogre tale (22, 23, 197, and 205).

As Rosa's narrative nears the moment when Sutpen made the proposition that drove her from his house, she pares down her set of literary models. We hear no more of tragedy. She disclaims the fairy tale: Sutpen, she says, was only a "childhood" ogre (205 and 208). The Sutpen who rode back from the war was "not the ogre" though "villain true enough, but a mortal fallible one less to invoke fear than pity" (209). Her narrative, then, retains its Gothic elements. She had seen herself as the innocent maiden; and Sutpen, as the madman, even the villain, whom she had served and yearned to save. She had imagined him as a man struggling "through a swamp with nothing to guide or drive him—no hope, no light: only some incorrigibility of undefeat." She had then believed that she could be his "sun" and give him light and hope. She had, however, also thought him mad—"Yes, mad, yet not so mad. . . . If he was mad, it was only his compelling dream which was insane and not his methods" (207). (Her remark obviously doesn't sanction all that Sutpen has done. In its context it means only that no madman could have avoided the Klan and made Wash

Jones work.) At this point she comes her closest to understanding Sutpen when she asks herself, "Why may it be not even madness but solitary despair in titan conflict with the lonely and fore-doomed and indomitable iron spirit?"

As the Gothic ingenue she had dreamed of shielding his madness to give him "airy space and scope" for his delirium (209–10). Here, however, as she recognizes but as some readers haven't, the Gothic romance collapses. Sutpen needed no shield. Sutpen made his proposition coolly, rationally: he asked her for a son. Rosa, who had seen herself as the heroine of a Gothic romance, then discovered her delusion. She had, she told Quentin, tried to pro-tect and save a demon: "He was not articulated in this world. He was a walking shadow. He was the light-blinded bat-like image of his own torment cast by the fierce demoniac lantern up from be-neath the earth's crust" (214). Rosa has proved unprepared for the quest she had set for herself and unwilling to complete it. In re-fusing it and retreating to Jefferson, she has discovered herself to be the heroine of a failed quest and thus of what we might call a Gothic irony. She remains trapped in that irony for the next forty-three years, mulling over Sutpen's insult but unable to repay him for it; and although we never learn exactly why she goes out to Sutpen's Hundred with the ambulance, the explanation that Shreve offers is itself ironic: "Do you suppose it was because she knew what was going to happen when she told it, took any steps, that it would be over then, finished, and that hating is like drink or drugs and she had used it so long that she did not dare risk cutting off the supply, destroying the source. . . . But at last she did reconcile herself to it, for his sake, to save him, to bring him into town where the doctors could save him" (465). Shreve's words—which, to me at least, ring true—point up how this little quest, too, proves ironic. Rosa, again the heroine, is willing to sacrifice her pleasure in hating Sutpen for the virtuous goal of saving Henry. A bit like the knight setting out to rescue the dam-sel in distress, she plans the mission and, to ensure its success, strikes quickly under cover of darkness. But again she's unpre-pared. It's as if the knight Sir Rosa hadn't realized that the damsel Henry probably doesn't want rescuing and that the dragon Clytie would protect him by destroying him and herself as well. As a result Rosa loses doubly. Even in cutting off the source of her hatred, she doesn't save Henry; she destroys him. Her story, which she had come to see as ironic, remains so at its end.

In telling his version of the Sutpen story, Mr. Compson knows that he knows neither Sutpen's reason for rejecting Bon nor Henry's reason for killing him. Even so, Mr. Compson senses that the story is a tragedy with Thomas Sutpen as its hero. In that tragedy the characters are, Mr. Compson says, "people too as we are and victims too as we are, but victims of a different circumstance, simpler and therefore, integer for integer, larger, more heroic and the figures therefore more heroic too" (109–10). Behind Sutpen Mr. Compson sees the machinery of the tragedy and the tragic stage. As Sutpen's plantation and marriage flourish, Mr. Compson says that Sutpen was "unaware that his flowering was a forced blooming . . . and that while he was still playing the scene to the audience, behind him fate, destiny, retribution, irony—the stage manager, call him what you will—was already striking the set and dragging on the synthetic and spurious shadows and shapes of the next one" (87–88). As tragic heroes use their great powers in blindly pursuing their goals against still greater opposition, so does Sutpen. Mr. Compson describes Sutpen's "alertness for measuring and weighing event against eventuality, circumstance against human nature, his own fallible judgment and mortal clay against not only human but natural forces" (62). Mr. Compson, then, sees the Sutpen story as tragic—as "a horrible and bloody mischancing of human affairs" (125)—without fully appreciating how it is a tragedy.

As a narrator Sutpen himself plays two roles. Although one might expect him to seem an autobiographical narrator, saying, as it were, "Here is the story of my life," he never assumes that stance. General Compson, sitting by the campfire and listening to Sutpen's account, finds him oddly detached from his own biography. Sutpen turns out to be, first, simply a storyteller: "He was not talking about himself. He was telling a story. He was not bragging about something he had done; he was just telling a story about something a man named Thomas Sutpen had experienced, which would still have been the same story if the man had had no name at all, if it had been told about any man or no man over whiskey at night" (308–9).

Sutpen defines the kind of story he thinks is telling. He conceives of it as a quest. He doesn't use that term but describes how he discovered its narrative pattern when a teacher read to his class in school: "I learned little save that most of the deeds, good and bad both, . . . within the scope of man's abilities, had already been performed and were to be learned about only from books. So I listened . . . though I did not know that in that listening I was equipping myself . . . for what I should later design to do. . . . That was how I learned . . . that there was a place called the West Indies to which poor men went in ships and became rich, it didn't matter how, so long as that man was clever and courageous" (301–2). As Sutpen talks, General Compson notices in him the traits that usually mark the hero of an episodic, elementary quest-romance. Making Sutpen sound like the young King-Arthur-to-be, General Compson says that Sutpen's "destiny had fitted itself to him, to his innocence, his pristine aptitude for platform drama and childlike heroic simplicity" (307). Sutpen, indeed, often breaks his story into episodes. General Compson found this narrative practice disturbing enough to comment on. As Quentin reports, Sutpen "just said that he was now engaged to be married and then he stopped telling it. He just stopped, Grandfather said, flat and final like that, like that was all there was, all there could be to it, all of it that made good listening from one man to another over whiskey at night" (319).

Sutpen's quest begins, as quests often do in romances, with a little boy compelled to take up a task he seems unprepared for: "All of a sudden he discovered, not what he wanted to do but what he just had to do . . . because if he did not do it he knew that he could never live with himself. . . . And that at the very moment when he discovered what it was, he found out that this was the last thing in the world he was equipped to do" (274–75). Getting turned away from the door calls Sutpen to his quest. He will seek to complete his design. Like other questers he must leave the settled, known world and pass into wild, alien spaces where he must endure and prevail in a series of adventures and tests. Sutpen sails to the West Indies, rises to oversee a plantation, and then faces a test, the rebellion and the slaves' siege of the plantation house where he and the planter, the planter's daughter, and two women servants have barricaded themselves in. At last, when their plight appears hopeless, Sutpen does what the hero of the quest-romance always does. Quentin repeats his grandfather's account of how Sutpen "put the musket down and went out and subdued them. That was how he told it: he went out and subdued them" (317). With this deed of valor he wins the maiden and gains riches. With the birth of a son, Sutpen should have completed the first stage of his quest. But he hasn't. The maiden and the son turn out not to be "adjunctive to the forwarding of the design" (327). Rather than having triumphed in the first stage, Sutpen has failed. The marriage has "made an ironic delusion of all that he had suffered and endured in the past and"—a bit of foreshadowing—"all that he could ever accomplish in the future toward that design" (328). Ironically, too, his quest is almost back where it was when he stood on a Tidewater wharf seeking a ship bound for the West Indies. Except that he now has money, his years in Haiti have been "wasted" (330).

Again, Sutpen sets out on a journey into the wild, passes tests, and appears to have triumphed when he has a prosperous plantation and a son. But again Sutpen's seeming triumph in his quest's first stage collapses. This collapse, of course, doesn't leave him standing on the wharf once more. He still has a wife, a daughter, property, and position. Nonetheless, his design has suffered a double setback. Henry has gone to New Orleans; and, perhaps worse, Sutpen sees that he must face his dilemma: either he takes Bon in, fulfilling the design publicly but actually betraying it, or he tells Henry enough to make Henry kill Bon, protecting the possibility of someday completing the design. Ironically, Sutpen's seeming triumph has turned into his most difficult test.

The Civil War, which amounts to another journey, allows him to postpone acting; but its approaching end compels Bon and Sutpen to reach their decisions. After Henry has slain Bon and disappeared, Sutpen once more needs to regain ground. By this time he may realize as we surely do that he is not the hero of a quest-romance but much more the blinded butt of its reverse, the ironic quest in which the hero fails to attain his goal.

Nevertheless, he rises to meet new tests. Needing another wife, he proposes to Rosa; and she accepts. Needing to reestablish Sutpen's Hundred, he struggles to keep whatever land he can. On the day when he finds out that he can "at least retain the shell of Sutpen's Hundred even though a better name for it would now be Sutpen's One" (210), he makes his proposition to Rosa. Her outraged refusal sets him back again. He has failed once more; he must find another woman.

This test requires no journey but consumes Sutpen's time. When Milly bears a girl, Sutpen, believing himself unable to father another child, sees that he can never attain his design. So he sets himself one final goal and at long last succeeds: he makes

Wash kill him. His ironic story, which he had at first taken for quest-romance, has come to its bleak end.

As storyteller at the campfire Sutpen seems scarcely aware that his tale might not be a quest-romance. But when he talks to General Compson during the war, Sutpen has learned otherwise and is no longer the storyteller. He is "trying hard to explain now because now he was old and knew it, knew it was being old that he had to talk against: time shortening ahead of him that could and would do things to his chances and possibilities" (325). In giving "the clear and simple synopsis of his history" (329), Sutpen is surely trying to understand his own plight. He may be offering the synopsis to General Compson partly in the hope that "the legal mind might perceive and clarify" what Sutpen believes to have been his mistake (341). General Compson, however, thinks that Sutpen is mainly "trying to explain to circumstance, to fate itself, the logical steps by which he had arrived at a result absolutely and forever incredible" (328–29), at the ironic dilemma that has him trapped. Either course he decides on, he tells General Compson, will destroy his design; and yet time is compelling him to act. As he gives General Compson the synopsis, Sutpen has abandoned storytelling in order to present the crux of his problem. He is the narrator as pragmatic analyst: he is narrating as a way to decide what to do. His analysis works. Even General Compson, who doesn't understand exactly what problem Sutpen is posing, comes close to recognizing how Sutpen will solve it; for the general says that Sutpen's "morality . . . would not permit him to malign or traduce the memory of his first wife . . . not even to his son by another marriage in order to preserve the status of his life's attainment and desire, except as a last resort" (339). More important, the analysis works for Sutpen, but only in the short run. When he leaves the general's office, Sutpen seems to have decided on his next step: that he must resort to telling Henry that Bon's mother and Bon are black. With that decision Sutpen's narrative roles conclude. At first as a storyteller he had conceived of his account as a quest-romance; but as it darkened into irony, he shifted to pragmatic analysis, which seemed to solve his immediate problem of what to do next but nonetheless carried him on, as he by then foresaw, to his and his story's ironic end.

Shreve begins his participation as a narrator not by telling a story but by asking Quentin for one: "Tell about the South.

What's it like there. What do they do there. Why do they live there. Why do they live at all" (218). The absence of question marks is, I think, significant. Despite the sentences' interrogative form, Shreve isn't asking questions. He's giving commands because he thinks he knows "about the South." He expects a story that will confirm his notions. (Likewise, many of Faulkner's readers have expected *Absalom* to confirm their views. As we'll see in the next chapter, that expectation has misled them.) And as the third-person narrator points out, this is "not Shreve's first time" (218); he already knows some of the story he is asking for, and from the next half-dozen pages we can infer the kind of story he thinks it is.

We can make that inference because, since Quentin declines to narrate, Shreve starts telling the story he wants to hear. It is not historical, biographical, or sociological, nor is it even a realistic fictional portrayal of "What it's like there." Instead, Shreve creates his story by letting his imagination "play" (349) over what he has learned from Quentin. His tone leaps back and forth between ironic understatement, which knowingly oversimplifies and debases motives, and ironic overstatement, which stems from elaborate, elevated allusions: "If [Sutpen] hadn't been a demon his children wouldn't have needed protection from him and [Rosa] wouldn't have had to go out there and be betrayed by the old meat and find instead of a widowed Agamemnon to her Cassandra an ancient stiff-jointed Pyramus to her eager though untried Thisbe" (222). Shreve never pauses between those leaps to describe people as people. Sutpen is both "a jackal" scuttling into a rockpile and, in an odd compound allusion, "this Faustus, this demon, this Beelzebub"; his slaves are "twenty subsidiary demons"; his neighbors are "the local ducal houses" and "the lesser baronage"; Henry and Judith and their unborn offspring, a "living bulwark between him (the demon) and the Creditor's bailiff hand" (223–24).

Eventually Shreve cools his narrative as he repeats to Quentin what Quentin has learned from his own experience, from his father, or from General Compson and has told Shreve. But Shreve never settles down to reportage or even realism but continues to color his story. The octoroon's visit to Bon's grave "must have resembled a garden scene by the Irish poet, Wilde"; at the grave stood the little Charles Etienne "whom Beardsley might not only have dressed but drawn" (241–42). When Clytie brings the boy, now orphaned, to live at Sutpen's Hundred, Shreve's metaphors make the child both little Lord Fauntleroy and "the delicate and perverse spirit-symbol, immortal page of the ancient immortal Lilith" (246).

As the next chapter begins, Shreve consolidates his narrative stance in three sentences, still without question marks: "Jesus, the South is fine, isn't it. It's better than the theatre, isn't it. It's better than Ben Hur, isn't it" (271). He believes that he is telling a story that reveals the South even more dramatically than *Ben Hur* revealed Rome. One might agree if one could add "and even less accurately"; for the story, as he conceives it, is as highly colored as Rosa's account. His ironic tone may serve to redeem his story; but, of course, her firsthand knowledge helped redeem hers. In short, Shreve doesn't want to know about the South; he wants a story better than *Ben Hur*. To want such a story is no mean ambition. Faulkner surely wanted to tell one; and we'd be reading *Ben Hur* ourselves if we didn't want to hear something better.

Nevertheless, Shreve's desire for a dramatic romance that will reveal the South deafens him to the tragic irony of Thomas Sutpen. The story of Sutpen differs so utterly from Shreve's expectations that he hardly recognizes it as a story in itself. Consequently, he looks further into the family's history and tries to discover or create there the kind of story he wants. That effort meshes well, as we shall see, with Quentin's own aims. Together, then, the two boys hardly hear themselves tell the story of Thomas Sutpen but refocus on his children and, by beginning to find real motives, create the story of Bon, Henry, Judith, and Clytie. That story, with its strong elements of quest-romance, finally proves to be basically ironic: the questers Bon and Henry fail while in the background Judith (and Clytie) unwittingly and thus ironically complete something much like Sutpen's quest and while Clytie, again ironically, destroys Henry and herself to protect him from those who have brought the ambulance to save him. The boys' narrative success draws in the third-person narrator to give the last details that clinch their interpretation. And we readers can then append their ironic account to the ironic tragedy of Thomas Sutpen.

Shreve gives his story the ending that has puzzled many a reader; but since Quentin's narrative concludes along with Shreve's, let's work our way through Quentin's first and then examine how both their narratives reach their endings. By asking Quentin to call on her, Rosa summons him to hear the Sutpen story or, more accurately, to hear it again; for plainly it has already interested him: before she speaks, one Quentin says to the other that Sutpen had died "without regret . . . save by her . . . and by Quentin Compson" (6). Through about the first half of the book he listens to Rosa and to his father partly to satisfy his curiosity by hearing more of the story and partly out of a practical interest in figuring out what Rosa wants him to do. Yet at the end of chapter 5 we discover that Quentin has not been listening to her because of "something which he . . . could not pass." The third-person narrator again conjures up the scene: the shot, Henry's running feet on the stairs, and Judith in her underthings snatching up her wedding dress as Henry bursts in, "the pistol still hanging against his flank." He and Judith speak in "staccato sentences like slaps":

> Now you cant marry him.
> Why cant I marry him?
> Because he's dead.
> Dead?
> Yes. I killed him. (215)

The narrator reiterates that Quentin has not heard what Rosa has said because he "couldn't pass" that scene (216). And that evening, according to the narrator, Quentin misses part of his father's account because Quentin "had something which he still was unable to pass" (218–19). That scene implies relationships among Bon, Judith, and Henry; and those relationships so fascinate Quentin that they give the rest of his narrative its impetus. Months later Mr. Compson's letter saying that Rosa has died revives the puzzle of the relationships.

Quentin, however, does not take the letter's arrival as an occasion to leap into solving the puzzle. When Shreve urges him to "tell about the South" (218), Quentin remains silent; and so Shreve has to do his own telling throughout chapter 6. When Shreve is narrating, Quentin resists getting drawn in. He mentally dismisses Shreve's account as nothing new—"He sounds just like Father" (227)—and, ignoring Shreve, recalls how Sutpen died. Shreve keeps talking for half a dozen pages, retelling Quentin's own story of visiting the Sutpen graveyard. The name *Judith,* however, stirs Quentin to imagine that after Bon's death she was "not bereaved" and so "did not need to mourn." The next thought that comes to him, though, is a protest at his fascination with the relationships. "Yes, I have had to listen too long" (243). That protest recurs several times (259–60 and 263); unwillingly but inexorably, Quentin is being drawn in. As chapter 6 ends, Shreve has carried the story up to the moment when Rosa and Quentin went out to Sutpen's Hundred, found only Clytie and Jim Bond, but "went on: and there was?" Quentin's "Yes" makes Shreve fear that Quentin may destroy the pleasure of the storytelling by answering the question immediately. "Wait then," Shreve cries. "For God's sake wait" (270).

In chapter 7 Quentin does wait, but he begins to talk. He takes up neither the question "And there was?" nor the relationships but tells of Sutpen's design. Quentin speaks in a "voice level, curious, a little dreamy yet still with that overtone of sullen bemusement, of smoldering outrage" (272). Throughout the chapter the third-person narrator keeps underscoring Quentin's "flat, curiously dead voice" (322), his "almost sullen flat tone" (319), and his attitude of "brooding" (343) and "brooding bemusement" (297). Quentin is stalling, keeping away from the relationships that so fascinate him; but now he is himself embroiled in the narrative. He will not be able to rest until he has perceived the passions that bind and separate Bon, Henry, and Judith.

Just after Quentin has told Shreve that Sutpen had planned to take in the nameless stranger, Shreve urges Quentin to "go on. Sutpen's children. Go on." Quentin replies, "Yes. The two children," and pauses. Shreve is pushing him toward describing the relationships that both attract and frighten him. In an interior monologue Quentin offers an analogy to explain why the Sutpen story fascinates him: "Maybe nothing ever happens once and is finished. Maybe happen is never once but like ripples maybe on water after the pebble sinks." And what happens to one person affects others: "the ripples moving on, spreading, the pool attached by a narrow umbilical water-cord to the next pool which the first pool feeds, has fed, did feed." The others feel the happening's effect even if they differ greatly from the person to whom the happening occurred: "Let this second pool contain a different temperature of water, a different molecularity of having seen, felt, remembered, reflect in a different tone the infinite unchanging sky, it doesn't matter: that pebble's watery echo whose fall it did not even see moves across its surface too" (326). Consequently, since the ripples from any pool spread over all the pools linked to it, Quentin sees that people are linked by happenings they never experienced directly—by, for instance, the story of the Sutpens. Thus he and Shreve "are both Father. Or maybe Father and I are both Shreve, maybe it took Father and me both to make Shreve or Shreve and me both to make Father or maybe Thomas Sutpen to make all of us" (326–27). Sutpen may have been the pebble that fell.

Through that analogy Quentin nears the relationships; yet the analogy also insulates him from them. He continues to tell about Sutpen until Shreve interrupts to get Quentin to focus on how Sutpen returned home and learned that Henry had killed Bon. Shreve is again pushing Quentin toward the relationships; and so this time it's Quentin who says, in a voice "tense suffused restrained," "Wait. . . . Wait, I tell you!" He then declares that he has taken control of the narrative: "I am telling" (345). He realizes that he must now speak of what Bon, Judith, and Henry felt. He does so at last, but only briefly. After half a page he returns to Sutpen.

Nevertheless, Quentin must know by now that he is bound to overcome his reluctance and that he will, along with Shreve, try to share the Sutpen children's feelings. To show that the two boys are now becoming allies in getting the story told, the third-person narrator points out that they both camouflage with levity their "youthful shame of being moved." That shame, the narrator adds, is "the reason for Quentin's sullen bemusement" (349). Quentin knows that the ripples from Bon's, Henry's, and Judith's pools will roil his. In telling their story, he will embarrass himself by stirring up his own emotions.

As chapter 8 begins, Quentin and Shreve—now joined in trying to perceive the passions that bound Bon, Judith, and Henry—are imagining a noble story of "honor" and "love" (369). As Quentin and Shreve come together, "curious and quiet and profoundly intent," they look at one another "almost as a youth and a very young girl might out of virginity itself—a sort of hushed and naked searching" (374). That sexual simile gets extended as the chapter continues. Quentin and Shreve are "creating between them . . . people" who play the roles in the story (378–79). Ultimately Quentin and Shreve unite in their "happy marriage of speaking and hearing . . . in order to overpass to love," to a narrative union in which "there might be paradox and inconsistency but nothing fault nor false" (395).

Their subject is love and honor, and Shreve is speaking of the
relationship between Judith and Bon when Quentin keeps objecting that it is "not love" (402 and 410). So far he has found no
reason to change his view that Judith did not mourn for Bon because she was not bereaved (243). What Quentin has seen by the
end of chapter 8, however, has compelled him to change his mind.
Within those thirty-eight pages he and Shreve (and the third-
person narrator) have constructed a narrative that contained
"nothing fault nor false." The chapter ends with the explanation
of why Bon had replaced Judith's picture in the locket with a picture of the octoroon and their child. Shreve, as the narrator, demands Quentin's concurrence: "I know. And you know too. Dont
you? Dont you, huh? . . . Dont you know? It was because he said
to himself, 'If Henry dont mean what he said, it will be all right;
I can take it out and destroy it. But if he does mean what he said,
it will be the only way I will have to say to her, *I was no good; do
not grieve for me.*' Aint that right? Aint it? By God, aint it?" And
Quentin replies, "Yes" (448).

What has he learned? Whatever it is, it has affected him profoundly because, in the opening of chapter 9, he begins "to jerk
all over, violently and uncontrollably" (450). Many critics, knowing Quentin's role in *The Sound and the Fury,* have said that what
disturbs him is seeing in Henry's and Bon's relationship with Judith an image of his own with Caddy. The critics' belief, of
course, rests on two main pieces of evidence in *Absalom*—some
phrases matching Quentin with Henry and Bon and the words
"pure and perfect incest" (119) to characterize the relationships
among Henry, Judith, and Bon. Yet that evidence requires at least
three qualifications: (1) The narrator pairs Quentin specifically
with Henry only once and then for only half a page (417). Every-
where else the narrator also matches Shreve with Henry and Bon;
and no one infers from that matching that Shreve has incestuous
feelings too. (2) The phrase about incest comes first from Mr.
Compson. If Faulkner means to make *Absalom* congruent with
The Sound and the Fury, then Mr. Compson's discussion of Henry's
possibly incestuous feelings is tactless and peculiar. It occurs, after
all, in the September just after the summer in which, according to
The Sound and the Fury, Quentin had tried to mislead his father by
falsely confessing to incest. Yet neither father nor son seems aware
of an analogy between Henry or Bon and Quentin. (3) Talk of

incest occurs often in chapter 8. The third-person narrator describes "Henry citing himself authority for incest, talking about his Duke John of Lorraine" (432); and near the chapter's end, in the italicized passage in the present tense, the narrator reports that Bon challenges Henry with "So it's the miscegenation, not the incest, which you cant bear" (445). Yet Quentin never alludes to incest in his own descriptions of Henry's and Bon's feelings, not even in his interior monologues.

Those qualifications imply that Quentin's feelings for Caddy have little to do with what makes him shiver—that is, with what he has learned. If he found the potential for incest fascinating, we would, I think, hear something about it directly from him through remarks to Rosa, Mr. Compson, or Shreve or through his interior monologues. At the very least we would expect the third-person narrator to bring it up. That we hear nothing from any of those sources reduces the likelihood that those feelings—ones that he had spoken of, perhaps invented, during the previous summer—are now making him shake. Since works of literature generally go far toward explaining themselves, perhaps we need not leave *Absalom* to discover what Quentin has learned and why it affects him so.

He has learned what he needed to understand to "pass" the scene in which Henry burst into Judith's bedroom. Quentin has discovered why Henry killed Bon and why Bon drove Henry to kill him. But that discovery has hardly proved satisfying. As Shreve wanted a story better than *Ben Hur,* so Quentin was looking for a story of love and honor. Both young men sought stories that would look into the heart of life and reveal "the immortal brief recent intransient blood which could hold honor above slothy unregret and love above fat and easy shame" (369).

In the story of the Sutpen children, however, they have found nothing so heroic. Neither *love* nor *honor* adequately fits the story's intricacies of motive. Judith, Bon, and Henry feel emotions that are not only more subtle but also less noble than pure love and honor; and Quentin and Shreve are disappointed—no, Quentin is appalled—at what finally moves Bon and Henry. From Bon's changing the picture in the locket, Quentin has surmised that Judith loved Bon and that Bon knew it. If *love* were too strong a word for Judith's feeling, she was certainly so smitten that she would not let mere honor stand in her way. According to Shreve, she would have said to herself, "I will do anything he might ask me to do and that is why he will never ask me to do anything that I consider dishonorable" (412). How, then, must Quentin judge Bon's final decision? Henry tries to appeal to Bon's feelings for Judith, their half sister. Henry says, "Think of her. Not of me: of her." But Bon replies, "I have. For four years. Of you and her. Now I am thinking of myself" (446). He is, in the end, putting the interests of his own ego above whatever love he might feel, whether fraternal for Judith and Henry or sexual for Judith. Like Sutpen himself, Bon will sacrifice others to his design; but unlike Sutpen's design, Bon's has merely personal, not societal, meaning and seeks no moral consequences that would measure up to opening the door to the nameless stranger. Dashing and sensitive and Byronic as he may be, Bon finally fails to deserve the admiration or even the respect of Quentin and Shreve as they seek heroes to look up to.

Nor can they look up to Henry. When he finds himself driven to prevent Bon from marrying Judith, Bon offers Henry a pistol and says, "Then do it now." Henry can't. "You are my brother," he says, appealing to his own fraternal feelings as he had appealed to Bon's feelings for Judith. And as Bon ignored that appeal, so does Henry. Instead, Henry listens to Bon's own words: "No I'm not. I'm the nigger that's going to sleep with your sister. Unless you stop me, Henry" (446). Henry listens because Bon is echoing the voice that speaks from the depths of Henry's being, from the depths that can accept incest but not miscegenation. Although Henry does not bring himself to slay Bon until they reach Sutpen's Hundred, Bon's words echo the order that Henry finally obeys. Thus, Quentin and Shreve have not told themselves the heroic love story they wanted to hear; instead, they have revealed a history in which love and honor fall prey to self-centeredness and racism.

No wonder, then, that Quentin shivers and that Shreve is puzzled. Shreve is still hoping that the Sutpen story will reveal the South: "I just want to understand it if I can. . . . Because it's something my people haven't got. Or if we have got it, it all happened long ago across the water and so now there aint anything to look at every day to remind us of it. . . . What is it? something you live and breathe in like air? a kind of vacuum filled with wraithlike and indomitable anger and pride and glory at and in happenings that occurred and ceased fifty years ago?" (450). Quentin tells Shreve, "You cant understand it. You would have to

be born there." Quentin's words have convinced a surprising number of critics, who have failed to see that, unless they themselves
were "born there," Quentin has disqualified them along with
Shreve. Shreve himself challenges Quentin by asking, "Do you
understand it?" Quentin vacillates "I dont know," he says. "Yes,
of course I understand it. . . . I dont know" (451).

Quentin comes to realize that being born there does not en-
tail understanding; and, indeed, we've seen that he himself does
not understand the story of the Sutpens. Perhaps, too, those of us
born elsewhere can understand the *it* that the boys are speaking
of. Probably a phrase like "the southern sense of the past" would
serve as an antecedent for *it*. Certainly, people born elsewhere can't
easily appreciate the force the past exerts on southerners. But a
sense of the past is too vast and too vaporous to explain the story
of the Sutpens. No moral, no neat tags will close *Absalom*. One
needs to pay attention to the evidence, to weigh it, to imagine
what the Sutpens felt, to infer motives, to gauge consequences.

In chapter 9 Quentin and Shreve, despite their disappoint-
ment at the end of the previous chapter, are continuing to try to
do all that; but they are no longer thinking as one. Their analytical
alliance is falling apart. Shreve follows Quentin's "I dont know"
with a challenge: "Yes. You dont know. You dont even know
about the old dame, the Aunt Rosa." Quentin answers, "No"
(451); but the challenge arouses his memory of going to Sutpen's
Hundred with her. The third–person narrator tells the story in
Quentin's voice and as Quentin remembers it; but although the
story lasts about eighteen pages, Shreve never hears it. And Quentin's memories seem to have flicked by in an instant, for Shreve's
next sentences reflect no passing of time. He asks why Rosa
waited three months before returning to Sutpen's Hundred to get
Henry, but Quentin does not answer. Lying "still and rigid" although his blood is running warm, Quentin is thinking "Nevermore of peace. Nevermore. Nevermore. Nevermore" (465).
Shreve's attempt to answer his own question stirs Quentin's
thoughts, this time not to remember but to imagine how Henry
and Clytie died in the flaming house. But again Shreve hears nothing from Quentin, who is staring silently at the window, which
turns into his father's letter telling of Rosa's death and burial.

At this point Quentin and Shreve are far apart. Shreve, still
conceiving the story as one about the South, takes refuge in bitter
humor. "The South," he says. "Jesus. No wonder you folks all

outlive yourselves by years and years and years." In contrast, Quentin is trying to read the end of his father's letter. He does not respond to its tone, which the narrator calls "whimsical" and "ironic" (469) and which sounds notes of optimism. Quentin cannot respond because, in coming to understand the scene in the bedroom, he has experienced a bitter, painful revelation: he has seen that Bon was selfish, that Henry was a racist who could accept incest but recoiled at miscegenation, and that both Bon and Henry had chosen to sacrifice their sister to their own ends. After that revelation Quentin believes he will nevermore be at peace.

As *Absalom* ends, Shreve is trying to concoct an ending that he thinks appropriate to a tale of the South. His bitter humor has now turned into cynicism and a passionate desire to end the story, no matter how. He cooks up a sort of moral, a closing principle, which manifestly doesn't fit: "So it takes two niggers to get rid of one Sutpen" (470). And, ostensibly from the Sutpen story, he foolishly projects a view of the future: "The Jim Bonds are going to conquer the western hemisphere . . . in a few thousand years." Finally, and typically, he asks Quentin, "Why do you hate the South?" Critics have spent quite a lot of ink debating whether Quentin hates the South. Quentin, on the contrary, has his answer ready: "I dont hate it." The narrator leaves no doubt about how readily the answer comes: Quentin speaks "quickly, at once, immediately" and repeats, "I dont hate it." The narrator then adds: "*I dont hate it* he thought, panting in the cold air, the iron New England dark: *I dont. I dont! I dont hate it! I dont hate it!*" (471). Shouldn't that many denials convince critics that he means what he says? Or does he protest too much? That debate continues because *Absalom* offers insufficient evidence to settle the issue. The book lacks the evidence because the issue is irrelevant. What matters is not what Quentin feels about the South but what he feels about the Sutpens.

5
Readers' Designs

ALTHOUGH WE CAN NOW CLAIM to understand Sutpen's design, the narration, the fabula, the characters' designs, and those of the narrators, a puzzle remains. Why have so many astute readers gone astray? Why have they failed to understand Sutpen's design although he (and Faulkner) expressed it in fairly straightforward words? And why have so many readers underestimated, or utterly failed to notice, the role of the third-person narrator in authenticating the climactic scene when Sutpen tells Henry that Bon is partly black? On the testing ground of *Absalom* the critics have plainly had a trying time. Their trials should arouse our curiosity: when the best readers have trouble, we need to know why. Their struggles might show how we too misuse our interpretive strategies and fall short of understanding important things about what works mean.

Absalom is, of course, inherently hard to interpret. Its narrators are numerous, overlapping, and usually unreliable. They even have differing notions about the kind of story they are telling. The plot is complex; the fabula is difficult to construct; the rhetoric is elaborate. Those designs are intricate enough to make interpretation troublesome.

On the other hand, critics earn their keep by solving interpretive difficulties of exactly those kinds. *Absalom* must, then, pose special interpretive problems. In fact, almost every literary

work poses its own challenges, challenges that contribute to drawing us to literature in the first place. As Jonathan Culler has said:

> We are attracted to literature because it is obviously some-
> thing other than ordinary communication; its formal and
> fictional qualities bespeak a strangeness, a power, an orga-
> nization, a permanence which is foreign to ordinary
> speech. Yet the urge to assimilate that power and perma-
> nence or to let that formal organization work upon us re-
> quires us to make literature into a communication, to
> reduce its strangeness, and to draw upon supplementary
> conventions which enable it, as we say, to speak to us. The
> difference which seemed the source of value becomes a dis-
> tance to be bridged by the activity of reading and interpre-
> tation. The strange, the formal, the fictional, must be
> recuperated or naturalized, brought within our ken, if we
> do not want to remain gaping before monumental inscrip-
> tions. . . .
>
>   To assimilate or interpret something is to bring it
> within the modes of order which culture makes available.[1]

To understand *Absalom*, then, we readers must place it within
at least one "mode of order": we must find a design in the work
or give it a design. Our urge to do so is compelling; for until we
have discovered a design in the work or assigned a design to it, we
will feel as ill at ease before it as before an enigma. To begin to
understand (and to gain security), we must entertain some hypothesis about the work's design: "It looks to me," we may say to
ourselves, "as if this work is a first-person narrative" or "a realistic
novel" or "an allegory about the South." In fact, fitting a work
within just one mode of order, one design, sometimes hardly suffices. We will need enough designs to encompass all the work's
details that seem to need accounting for. Whatever designs we
choose will be abstractions from the work: some of its details will
necessarily get omitted. Our choosing to emphasize, say, five particular designs makes us confront a dilemma. We don't want to
overlook a crucial detail; but, on the one hand, we need to have a
design in mind to know which details are crucial; and, on the
other, we need to know which details are crucial before we can
wisely choose a design. From its title and its first words (where

1. Culler, 134 and 137.

interpretation always begins), *Absalom* offers such challenges that one might almost regard it as a readers' testing ground. This chapter, then, will look at the designs readers have found in *Absalom* or brought to it and at the designs that readers have sometimes had on it.

Theory as Design:
Derrida, Barthes, Burke, Cassirer, and Freud

Some readers have imported designs from far away, most recently by deploying concepts borrowed from Jacques Derrida, Michel Foucault, and Roland Barthes. David Krause, for example, says: "That written texts endure for Faulkner (as for Foucault) as uniquely coded monumental documents . . . means that their most complete reading must be one that works hard (yet relaxes enough) to remain acutely sensitive to the intricate, ceaseless play of signification. . . . That no one reading can accomplish such exhausting, exhaustive work means that rereading becomes possible, in fact necessary."[2] Here Krause has pointed out where I think the most readers trip up: on *Absalom*'s demand for careful reading and rereading. Few readers have proved willing to give *Absalom* such exhaustive attention.

Using Barthes's terms, Krause goes on to describe *Absalom* as a "pensive" text, one that keeps its ultimate meaning in suspension. Barthes shows that a pensive text responds best to what he calls a "'writerly' reading; that is, a reading fully open to the free play of signification . . . , unintimidated by the text's pensiveness but respectful of its reticences, its secrets. A 'readerly' reading, driving toward the (chimerical) security of coherence, stasis, mimesis, representation of what is signified, will not satisfy a genuinely pensive text."[3] While I am also contending against "readerly" readers who rush for coherence and stasis, *Absalom* seems to me to allow for more closure than "ceaseless play" implies. One might think that Krause is following the lead of many deconstructionists. Too often they are so busy demolishing meaning that a phrase like "ceaseless play of signification" turns into cant. Such a phrase suggests that the critic is revealing what is permanent ("ceaseless"), enjoyable ("play"), and meaningful ("signification"). Yet what we find such critics doing is continually revealing

2. Krause, "Reading Bon's Letter," 238.

3. Ibid., 239.

that no meaning is indubitable. That should come to no one as a surprise. Making that point again and again, as deconstructionists are doing, resembles the ceaseless play of bulldozers in a field of rubble.

Krause, however, is more subtle than that. He uses his argument not only to demolish constructed meanings but also, in the end, to clear the ground to give readers a chance to "read *Absalom, Absalom!* 'better.'"[4] Even so, Krause's design, which makes the play of signification "ceaseless," may create for him a needless difficulty. The design he employs may preclude his seeing degrees of closure that exist. For Krause the third-person narrator is "unidentified, dislocated," holding "in no way a privileged place."[5] The deconstructive design takes that as axiomatic; and so when the third-person narrator catches fire and shifts to the present tense to tell of Henry's meeting Sutpen in his tent, Krause's design cannot note how much the narrator has gained a privileged place and introduced a firmer closure. As a design, deconstruction thus proves too rigid, too determined that the play can never cease. Yet Krause uses that design well in calling for rereadings that might produce better readings and perhaps what he hyperbolically calls a "most complete" one. I would settle for the one that is most nearly so.

In *The Play of Faulkner's Language* Matthews, also following Derrida, wants to keep the signifiers in "infinite play." "The narratives of *Absalom* behave as rival offspring of the novel; the marriages of speaking and hearing issue in contending interpretations whose legitimacy or illegitimacy cannot finally be judged."[6] Making those judgements is usually difficult but seldom impossible. In Matthews's overstatement one hears the voice of the deconstructionist shouting at the signifiers, "Play, damn it, play." Matthews's design necessitates that they play endlessly around the book's two cruxes: What is Sutpen's design, and Why did Henry kill Bon? Because Matthews isn't looking for answers, he cannot recognize them when they appear. What we have found, though, is that while the narrative plays long around those cruxes, it finally goes much further toward solving them than Matthews's design will let him see.

4. Ibid.

5. Ibid., 234 and 235.

6. Matthews, 118 and 152.

Walter Brylowski analyzes *Absalom* through the concept of the four levels of myth that he derives from Ernst Cassirer and Joseph Campbell. Brylowski gives a concise catalogue of the biblical and classical allusions and analogies that make up his first level of myth. On the second level he finds a "mythos" of action and plot in "the rise and fall of Thomas Sutpen in terms of his 'design' and, on a larger, allegorical level, the flaw in the design of the antebellum South. . . . The flaw is quite apparent: the moral failure of Negro-white relations." Brylowski's notion of the design, however, has Sutpen accepting the Tidewater world's dynastic vision. According to Brylowski, Sutpen accepts it because he does not use reason to see the world as it is. Sutpen thereby participates in myth's third level, a nonrational and nonempirical mode of perception and thought. Brylowski's misinterpretation of Sutpen's design vitiates this stage of his argument. And even if the argument were not vitiated, one could contend that Sutpen manages to succeed in a complicated world better than nonrational, nonempirical thinking would permit. Brylowski also locates similar thinking in the ways the narrators conceive of and tell their versions of the Sutpens' story and in the book's ultimate view. That view, Brylowski believes, is expressed in Quentin's repeatedly thinking that he does not hate the South. Brylowski proposes a fourth level, a "quasi-historical saga" that gives the historical "reality" of the South a "moral reading." In that saga what happens today derives from the past, and so evils today derive from "moral guilt . . . equated with exploitation of the land and of the Negro."[7] In these last stages of the argument I believe that Brylowski misrepresents the book. Nothing is so simple as he makes it sound. The narrators are more rational and empirical than he allows; Quentin's final words don't amount to the book's ultimate vision; no matter what happened in the South, *Absalom* does not show that Sutpen exploited the land; and we can't, I think, be sure that he was exploiting Negroes either. Brylowski is so intent on finding "myth" that he fails to read accurately.

From Cassirer and Kenneth Burke comes the design that Donald Kartiganer brings to *Absalom*. His essay "Process and Product" investigates what he calls an "irredeemably process condition" in which "no product may exist but the ones we create,

7. Brylowski, 21, 37, 38, 42, 39.

and each creation suffers the fallacies (which is to say the person-alities) of its creator."[8] That design, like deconstructionism, tends to conceal whatever closure the text may achieve; but unlike deconstructionism Kartiganer's design invites all of us to create our own forms of closure. Because he is focusing on the "process condition" in which readers make meaning, he cannot easily see meanings that seem to be awaiting discovery in the text, that at least seem to exist there independent of the process of making meaning.

Kartiganer introduces Cassirer's distinction between primitive "unity of being" and the "classification and systemization" of scientific thought to explain how Sutpen's boyhood view of the world changes when he moves from the mountains to Tidewater Virginia. But in Kartiganer's hands the distinction does not clarify Sutpen's behavior; and despite the freedom that Kartiganer's design grants, he discovers only the commonly held answers to the cruxes. He dismisses Sutpen's account of his design as "in many ways the most remote and meaningless of all" and sees that design as simply "a devoted belief" in the Tidewater social structure.[9]

In a later book Kartiganer develops his idea of Sutpen as a primitive man, an idea deriving from Cassirer. Kartiganer's account reveals why that idea has misled him. Sutpen, he writes, is "a literalist of the imagination, blind to the arbitrary nature of the symbols of society. To him the elements of social life—the house, the slaves, the wife, the son—have a magic power: phases of a ritual that is not symbolic but 'real.'"[10] Once he has conceived of Sutpen as a primitive, Kartiganer cannot see that Sutpen intends to strike out against society and its values. In Kartiganer's design no primitive could entertain so sophisticated an aim.

By importing Burke, Kartiganer wants to investigate the narrators' motives: "strategies of composition," he says, "are what *Absalom, Absalom!* is all about." He cites Burke's view that "the motivation out of which [the poet] writes is synonymous with the structural way in which he puts events and values together when he writes." Kartiganer argues that although "Burke is thinking of real poets," Burke's view applies equally well to "imaginary ones"

8. Kartiganer, "Process and Product," 801.

9. Ibid., 808, 807, 805, 806.

10. Kartiganer, *Fragile Thread*, 90.

like the narrators in *Absalom*. Taking Burke a step further, Kartiganer says, "Each version of the Sutpen history we receive . . . is
an exercise in symbolic extrication from some condition of anxiety." This assumption leads him into untenable positions. He must
see Mr. Compson as devising a narrative that will extract him
from anxiety, although in *Absalom* Mr. Compson says that his narrative is "incredible. It just does not explain" (124), hardly the
words of a man satisfied with his narrative's effects. Kartiganer's
assumption has to play down the third-person narrator: in com-
parison with characters, such narrators have little personality and
therefore may display little if any anxiety. Thus, although Kartiganer's essay and book both recognize that the third-person narrator exists, Kartiganer undervalues the narrator's role. The
passage that the essay describes as Quentin's and Shreve's cooper-
ative creation of "the deepest truth of the Sutpen story" actually
comes not from them but from the narrator.[11] And despite spending several pages asking how Quentin and Shreve know that Bon
is black, Kartiganer still never notices that it is the narrator who
answers that question.

The designs drawn from Burke's and Cassirer's theories, like
those from Derrida's and the others', have not encompassed
Faulkner's novel. Those theories are perhaps so foreign to *Absalom*
that they do not speak its language and so cannot interpret it. A
more promising source of designs is Sigmund Freud since so
much in *Absalom* concerns family relationships. André Bleikasten
uses Freud as a design for understanding both Sutpen's aim and
Quentin's fascination with the story of the Sutpens. The Freudian
design, however, is much better suited to analyzing relationships
within the family than to looking at relationships between indi-
viduals and society. As a result, I think, of that limitation, which
is inherent in his design, Bleikasten brushes aside any possibility
that Sutpen aims to do more than "to acquire land, to build a
stately mansion, to found a dynasty, i.e., to appropriate all the
attributes that defined social leadership in the Old South." Bleikasten writes that "instead of rebelling against the Southern ruling
class, young Sutpen decides to join it." But after excluding the
societal effect that Sutpen seeks, the Freudian design cannot stop
with conceiving Sutpen's dream as the "vulgar ambitions of the
parvenu." Bleikasten sets the quest within Sutpen's psyche: "To

11. Ibid., 72, 71, 72; "Process and Product," 813.

Sutpen it is not merely a matter of replacing one father by another, but of having no father at all, of being both one's own father and one's own son—*causa sui,* self-generated, self-enclosed, and self-sufficient. Sutpen is no god, but he would be god. Autogenesis." Bleikasten's Freudian design disregards much that is comparatively self-evident about Sutpen's attitudes. Sutpen recalls his father clearly without being either fixated on him or fixated on ignoring him. Rather than wanting to be his own son, he needs a son for the design and dies when he realizes that he will not get that son. Bleikasten writes that Sutpen "must deny his sons, for if he acknowledged them as sons he would have to abide by the law of patrilineal succession and to envision the transmission of his power to his descendants." Sutpen does not deny his "sons" in the plural; he denies Bon. Sutpen's design *will* violate patrilineal succession, and the transmission of power to the nameless stranger's descendants is exactly what Sutpen does envision. The Freudian design thus proves powerful enough to erase Sutpen's design as *Absalom* defines it and to create in its place another design altogether.

Just as Bleikasten's design overpsychologizes Sutpen, it overstates Quentin's role as the book's narrative consciousness. The design makes that overstatement possible because the Freudian model can penetrate characters more readily than it can analyze a characterless third-person narrator. For Bleikasten, then, Quentin becomes the "central narrative and interpretative voice" and "the tale's ultimate sender and receiver."[12] The design hardly seems able to perceive that the third-person narration exists, much less to recognize its role in the book.

The Freudian design, guided however by a closer reading of *Absalom* than Bleikasten's, enables T. H. Adamowski to develop one of the strongest interpretations of Sutpen's design. (Even in his hands, though, the design fails to reveal that the third-person narrator authenticates Bon's status.) Adamowski avoids many pitfalls simply by ignoring some of the common designs—designs that would, he mockingly says, link Sutpen to "the Tweed Ring, the New Deal, or logical positivism." Adamowski contends that *Absalom* uses what Freud called the family romance fantasy as a way to give Sutpen's design shape and meaning. "I do not mean to suggest that Sutpen 'has' a family romance fantasy, but only

12. Bleikasten, 140, 139, 140, 137, 138.

that the novel seems to include as a vehicle for Sutpen's design a narrative structure resembling the structure of the fantasy." When Sutpen gets turned away from the door, Adamowski says, the narrative manifests all the elements of the romance "at once: childhood harmony, discontent, the move to a new father who is ennobled with the old father's virtues, and the flight from both fathers in order to create a third with traces of both, Sutpen himself." Again, the Freudian design seems unable to reveal how Sutpen's aim would shock society. The design makes visible only the way his aim would affect his psyche. But Adamowski increases his design's analytical power by introducing a societal viewpoint through Jean-Paul Sartre's "*passion inutile* of man to be in-itself-for-itself." At the plantation owner's door Sutpen "sees himself, and through the gaze of another person his stability comes to an end in shame: 'Shame is by nature *recognition*. I recognize that I *am* as the Other sees me. . . .' [Sutpen] is overcome by a glance that reveals to him other points of reference than his own." Following Sartre, Adamowski says that Sutpen can "reclaim his 'selfness'" only by making himself able to look at the Other in turn. To attain that ability, according to Adamowski, Sutpen identifies with the aggressor and decides that he must "become one of 'them.'" His oneness must be flawless, Adamowski correctly explains, because "there must be nothing they or he (for he sees with *their* eyes) can see. A Sutpen family must be able to defuse looks." Adamowski sums up his argument by saying that "the quest for autonomy . . . conveyed in a way that is analogous to the fantasy of controlling one's own parentage, . . . serves as a vehicle for an ontological quest (to be the seen-seeing) which is the real meaning of Sutpen's design."[13]

Here Adamowski comes closer to identifying Sutpen's aim than does any other critic I have read: Sutpen's "design is meant to enable him, one day, to open his door to an 'amazed and desperate child,' so that the latter might in turn 'shut the door himself forever behind him on all that he had ever known.'" At that point in the explication, however, Adamoswki's design permits the psyche to dominate, allowing him to regard the boy at the door as only a "shadow" of Sutpen. Adamowski protests that "when an actual boy does come . . . , Sutpen does not allow Charles Bon to escape

13. Adamowski, "Children," 116, 118, 120, 116, 120–21, 121, 123, 125.

his past, but . . . inflicts it on him."[14] Because, in Adamowski's design, the psyche is the scene of the action, he seems unable to hear Sutpen's explanation that opening the door to Bon would have completed the design only "to the public eye" (342). Thus Adamowski finally does not grasp that Sutpen did not aim merely to become one of "them" so that he could once more see himself as "their" equal. No, Sutpen was, as he said, "fixing to combat them" (297).

The Faulkner Canon as Design

Instead of reading by the light of a theory—whether deconstructionist, structuralist, mythic, or psychoanalytic—some readers have taken the Faulkner canon as their design. By assuming coherence in either the canon or some subset of it, they have tried to use Faulkner's other works to interpret *Absalom*.

One way to go about establishing that coherence is to seek a theme that runs throughout the set of works. Walter J. Slatoff makes the most ambitious of such efforts when he argues that the overarching pattern in Faulkner's work is his "quest for failure." Slatoff finds that pattern in Faulkner's "ambiguity and irresolution," his "generally irrationalistic attitudes," his "discontent with the ability of language to convey truth," his "complex unresolved suspensions," his oxymorons, and "the intense contradictory feelings which, as much as anything else, . . . explain Faulkner's attitude toward life and toward his own art." Slatoff ultimately concludes that Faulkner was "determined to avoid clarifying or finishing his ideas, almost as though he feared to take hold of them, to give them full shape or realization, as though in some obscure way he wished to fail so that he would be able to go on trying."[15]

Believing that Faulkner found failure in *Absalom*, Slatoff says:

It is difficult to conceive of an "ending" that would provide less ordering and resolution. . . .

When we have finished the book . . . we feel . . . emotionally and intellectually bewildered. . . . We don't know to what extent we have watched a tragedy, the story

14. Ibid., 122.

15. Slatoff, 239, 241, 248, 250, 251, 260.

of a great man whose destruction of himself and his house is due essentially to flaws in character; to what extent a naturalistic drama in which morality and human guilt are irrelevant and the destruction a result of hereditary, economic, and social forces beyond the control of any of the characters; to what extent a grim and pointless joke to which the fitting commentary is the howling of the last Sutpen, who is an idiot.

The last two of his choices strike me as improbable readings. Slatoff could have strengthened his argument by mentioning far more common alternatives. But, I suggest, he is not eager to confront and clarify readings. With the "quest for failure" as a design, Slatoff will naturally find *Absalom* a "bewildering suspension of elements" impossible to interpret.[16] If it were not that to him, his design would instantly fail.

Richard P. Adams, whose *Faulkner: Myth and Motion* offers what I take as the best interpretation of *Absalom,* proposes a design that is both mythological and thematic. Unlike Brylowski, Adams finds myth a tool, but not the only tool, in Faulkner's workshop and so refrains from trying to make it explain everything. And the theme that Adams examines—that "life is motion" and that Faulkner meant his works to "arrest motion"—is native to Faulkner, not imported from outside. Here, too, Adams doesn't seek to make his design all-encompassing. His book's focus, he says, "is narrow and its approach is only one of many that may be profitable. But I believe that it strikes somewhere near the center of what Faulkner tried to do and did do."[17]

Adams succeeds in recognizing and quoting, even though he does not analyze, the passages that express Sutpen's design. Adams does not, I believe, actually understand that design: he concludes that Sutpen's story "epitomizes the history of the South." But Adams's judgment of why Sutpen fails, a judgment that derives from the theme "life is motion," rings more nearly true than any of the common ones. They hold that Sutpen fails because he's an egoist or a conformist or a rationalist or a racist. In Adams's view the South had made itself into "a static obstacle to the motion of life in the world"; likewise, Sutpen took on a

16. Ibid., 201–2, 199.

17. Adams, *Faulkner: Myth and Motion,* 3.

"static 'design'—the word is well chosen—which then defines his character and identity. It is a monomania which . . . will never let him become a man, with human feelings, human virtues, and a human capacity for the continual compromises imposed by human inconsistency, weakness, and error. Because he is unwilling or unable to bend, his doom in Faulkner's dynamic world is to be broken by the ubiquitous winds and floods of change." Although Adams seems to equate Sutpen and the South while I see him opposing it, Adams is surely right to see Sutpen's rigidity broken by the ironic dynamism of a world whose design brings Bon to his door.[18]

Adams is also astute in sizing up the third-person narrator, whom he calls "the author." In the climactic scene the italics mark "the complete intermingling of 'the two the four the two' (p. 346 [*AA:CT* 432])—or five with the author and six with the reader—into a single timeless moment of awareness." He concludes that "This awareness contains the whole experience of the book up to that point." Perhaps Adams goes too far toward making Quentin and Shreve seem to participate overtly in the narration. Apart from that, however, his account shows exactly why the scene is the climax.[19]

Adams's interpretation succeeds, in short, because his design, myth and particularly motion, grows out of Faulkner's work, because Adams makes his design flexible enough to fit the book's contours, and because he pays closer attention than many readers have paid to the words on the pages.

Apart from seeking a theme within the canon, readers may treat it or a part of it as a coherent whole in another way: they may try to make the characters in *Absalom* consistent with those in *The Sound and the Fury*. For example, Ragan finds *Absalom* "explicable" without presupposing canonical coherence. Yet he feels drawn toward *The Sound and the Fury*. At first its pull seems slight: some passages, he says, may be "puzzling if not interpreted in light of the earlier book"; having read it "immeasurably enriches the complexities of *Absalom, Absalom!*" Within two pages, however, Ragan's view has changed. The book that had seemed explicable by itself now is beginning to require *The Sound and the Fury*: "At more than one point [Quentin's] peculiar involvement in the

18. Ibid., 190–91, 214, 190.

19. Ibid., 196.

Sutpen story is practically incomprehensible to the reader unfamiliar with his reactions to events and concerns in the earlier novel." Ragan suggests that *Absalom* relies on *The Sound and the Fury* for the description we need of Shreve. Ragan even surmises that, although *Absalom* never mentions Caddy, the reader probably is expected to know of her: "That Caddy is never alluded to . . . does not indicate that Faulkner expects the reader to be unaware of the parallels between her and Judith. . . . the lack of direct reference to her is consistent with the author's practice throughout this most demanding of his novels. We are constantly forced to accept things which are not presented in the text itself." [20]

Such an approach may hardly seem to need defending. After all, when a Mr. Compson and his son Quentin both appear in two novels set in Jefferson, Mississippi, in the 1920s, a reader would seem justified in taking them as the same people with similar lives and outlooks from novel to novel. Other novels—by writers as diverse as Trollope, Farrell, Cooper, Proust, and Joyce—invite and reward that approach. In Faulkner's fiction, however, it is risky to assume that any set of works will fit a coherent history. Suratt turns into Ratliff; Horace Benbow, into Gavin Stevens. Characters with the same name change their natures, as Virginia Du Pre does between *Sartoris* and *Sanctuary* and as Mink Snopes does between the first two volumes of the trilogy and the last one. On the map at the end of *Absalom,* Faulkner asserted his power as Yoknapatawpha's "Sole Owner & Proprietor." "These people I figure belong to me," he said, "and I have the right to move them about in time when I need them." [21] "They're horses in my stable and I can run them whenever I want to." [22] He exercised his power in particular on Quentin Compson, as John W. Hunt has shown. Quentin dies in 1910 in *The Sound and the Fury,* published in 1929. In 1936 Faulkner used Quentin as a narrator for *Absalom,* which is set in the year before Quentin's death. Readers who have tried to make the two novels cohere have correctly found no obvious incoherence in Quentin's reappearance in *Absalom* because it was set earlier. But between those two publication dates—in 1931, to be exact—Faulkner published the short story "That Evening Sun." Quentin is its narrator, too; but the story is set in 1914, four years

20. Ragan, *William Faulkner's* Absalom, 18, 20, 88, 45.

21. Gwynn and Blotner, 79.

22. Blotner, 1309.

after his death in *The Sound and the Fury.* No reader, then, can assume biographical coherence in Faulkner's narratives about the Compson family.

To assume such coherence even between the novels demands justification. Many critics who assume that coherence take it, as Thomas Daniel Young does, as self-evident: "The reading I offer . . . is based on the following hypotheses: (1) that the Quentin Compson who appears as character and narrator in *Absalom, Absalom!* is the same youth who had the disturbing and destroying experiences related in *The Sound and the Fury,* and (2) that the narrative he creates in *Absalom, Absalom!* is vastly influenced by the impact these experiences had on him."[23] The hypotheses, however, need buttressing before they can support the weight of an argument. Because Faulkner resurrected Quentin in the short story, canonical coherence won't do. Even if we set the story aside and try to make the two novels fit together, we will see that Faulkner omitted from *Absalom* much that one might have expected to have been carried over from *The Sound and the Fury.* Where are Jason, Benjy, Mrs. Compson, Miss Quentin, and Dilsey? Where, above all, is Caddy? If the Sutpen story fascinates Quentin because he sees Caddy and himself in Judith, Henry, and Bon, why does Caddy's name never occur in the 471 pages?

A reader who notices such omissions but unquestioningly assumes coherence as a design may actually blame Faulkner for failing to complete that design. Jean-Jacques Mayoux says: "Quentin committed suicide at the end of *The Sound and the Fury.* It is perhaps an error of Faulkner's genius, to have linked the identity of that neurotic with the young man in *Absalom, Absalom!* . . . One needs, it seems to me, to forget the other Quentin while searching for the meaning of *Absalom, Absalom!* Our narrator [Quentin], however terrifying his nervous tension might be, should have made a nobler end, more stoical, more appropriate to his imagination."[24] Schoenberg, too, blames Faulkner for ignoring the design she has in mind: "I should like to have been able to explain the peculiar strategy by which Faulkner kept out of *Absalom, Absalom!* all reference to Caddy, the other characters, and all the events of *The Sound and the Fury.* Their absence forces too heavy reliance on awareness of the earlier novel. Unless the reader

23. Young, 83.

24. Mayoux, 167.

has recently experienced that novel and has it firmly in mind, the cost is too great."[25] Faulkner wasn't obliged to follow that design; nor is a reader obliged to expect it. Adopting coherence between the two novels as a design makes sense only if it produces better interpretations than other designs do. Here, then, we should consider Irwin, who makes the most vigorous attempt to use coherence as a design for understanding *Absalom.*

Irwin assumes that Faulkner's "novels are parts of a single continuing story," but he wants to analyze them as Freudians analyze dreams. Working back and forth between *The Sound and the Fury* and *Absalom,* Irwin seeks to "decipher a hidden story by analyzing the variations among the patent translations of that story, trying to discover the laws of condensation, distortion, substitution that govern the different oblique repetitions of that same hidden story." The story he discovers will therefore not be manifest but latent content. It will exist "in that imaginative space that the novels create *in between* themselves by their interaction. The analysis of one novel will not reveal it, nor will it be revealed by an analysis of all the novels in a process of simple addition, for since the structure is created by means of an interplay between texts, it must be approached through a critical process that, like the solving of a simultaneous equation, oscillates between two or more texts at once."[26] Irwin's design looks like a promising way to interpret *Absalom* by means of coherence. It seems to bypass mundane biographical coherence for a deeper latent coherence that only we subtle readers can discover.

Nevertheless, what is already manifest, I think, is that this design has its problems. It depends on "interplay between texts," but only the novels can play the game. Why has Irwin silently cut the short stories from the team? And if *Mosquitoes, A Fable,* and *Absalom* are all parts of any "single continuing story," Irwin must be giving the word *story* a most uncommon meaning. In any case, although he says that *all* the novels make a single story, he makes no effort to prove that claim. If we accept his sweeping hypothesis, however, it will authorize his bringing together *The Sound and the Fury* and *Absalom.* Once he places those novels, and only those novels, side by side, Quentin Compson, the main character they

25. Schoenberg, 11.

26. Irwin, 27, 3, 157–58.

have in common, will inevitably gain prominence: "The key to the critical oscillation . . . between *Absalom, Absalom!* and *The Sound and the Fury* is, of course, the figure of Quentin Compson— Quentin, whose own oscillation constantly transforms action into narration and narration into action."[27] When, for Irwin, Quentin looms large in *Absalom,* the Sutpens and their story must consequently fade. Once Quentin dominates the way Irwin sees the book, his design as canon transforms itself into biographical coherence. That transformation explains why "That Evening Sun" can't join in the intertextual interplay. Biographical coherence refuses to consider Quentin as both a twenty-year-old suicide and a twenty-four-year-old narrator.

By highlighting Quentin, the design inflates his role as a narrator and completely conceals the third-person narrator from Irwin: "There are, of course, four narrators in the novel—Quentin, his father, his roommate Shreve, and Miss Rosa Coldfield—but of these four certainly Quentin is the central narrator. . . . One reason that the voices of the different narrators sound so much alike is that we hear those voices filtered through the mind of a single listener: Quentin's consciousness is the fixed point of view from which the reader *overhears* the various narrators, Quentin included." Unable to hear the third-person narrator, Irwin gives Quentin credit for more than his own narrative accomplishments. Irwin writes that "surely, there can be no question that Quentin reconstructs the story of Bon, Henry, and Judith in the light of his own experiences with Candace and Dalton Ames." But there are, surely, some questions about that. First, Mr. Compson does much of that reconstruction. Next, Shreve seems to contribute to the construction by making inferences that go beyond what Quentin has told him. And finally the crucial scene that clarifies Bon's, Henry's, and Judith's motives and relationships comes not from Quentin but from the third-person narrator alone. Irwin's design, however, blocks out all that; and so he says, "Quentin and Shreve's identification with Henry and Bon . . . becomes so complete that Quentin and Shreve supply the missing information in the story with the authority of participants and not simply narrators."[28]

By insisting that *Absalom* must parallel Quentin's experience,

27. Ibid., 158.
28. Ibid., 26, 74, 76.

Irwin's design also underemphasizes the Sutpens' story: "Much of the story of Bon, Henry, and Judith, as Quentin imagines it, may simply be the return of Quentin's own repressed experiences with Candace and Ames." The design thus almost erases the Sutpens from his interpretation: "Of the many levels of meaning in *Absalom,* the deepest level is to be found in the symbolic identification of incest and miscegenation and in the relationship of this symbolic identification both to Quentin Compson's personal history in *The Sound and the Fury* and to the story that Quentin narrates in *Absalom, Absalom!*" Even when Irwin does try to attend to the Sutpens, his looking into the gap between the books sometimes diverts his attention from what *Absalom* itself says. Instead of heeding what the book says about Sutpen's design, for example, Irwin spends about six pages analyzing Faulkner's off-the-cuff remarks about it at the University of Virginia. Irwin then concludes that Sutpen set out to "vindicate the right of every poor white boy to an equal opportunity to become the rich planter, but . . . once he has vindicated that right by becoming the rich planter, he immediately denies that same right to black boys, specifically, to his black son Charles Bon." Irwin's design makes him generalize too quickly; he therefore lapses into inaccuracies and overstatements. Rosa and Quentin, he says, "are both virgins who have refused incest, Quentin with his sister, Rosa with her brother-in-law."[29] Neither example seems quite right. "Refused" sounds too strong for the scene in *The Sound and the Fury.* Quentin had hinted at incest; but when Caddy replied, "Ill do anything you want me to anything," Quentin told her, "You shut up."[30] Rather than refusing, Quentin weakly declined to carry out what he himself had suggested. And if sex with one's brother-in-law be incest, then when Rosa agreed to marry Sutpen, she agreed to incest. What she refused would be *extramarital* incest.

Again we can see Irwin trying to bend the book to his will when he says, "The result of Henry's murder of his black half brother is the kind of regression that one would expect from the suicidal murder of the double: Henry ends his life hidden in the womb of the family home." That comment skips so lightly from the murder to Henry's return that one might almost forget that

29. Ibid., 84, 25–26, 105, 75.

30. Faulkner, *The Sound and the Fury,* 194.

the two events may have been separated by roughly forty years. Such a regression is mighty slow. Yet another bending occurs when Irwin says that "Quentin's incestuous love for Candace is mirrored by Bon's love for Judith."[31] Granting what one need not grant—that Quentin feels incestuous love for Caddy—one might still object to Irwin's statement on two grounds. Do we know that Bon loves Judith? (We have looked at evidence that Quentin and Shreve think he doesn't love her enough.) And if Bon does love her, does his love resemble Quentin's for Caddy? Quentin kills himself because his childhood relationship with Caddy can't continue since she is outgrowing it. Bon has Henry kill him because Sutpen won't acknowledge him. Those situations and motives do not, I think, "mirror" one another.

Terms like *mirror* recur in Irwin's argument and cause it difficulties. He compares Quentin to Narcissus, who in "at least one version of the Narcissus myth . . . is rendered inconsolable by the death of his identical twin sister, and when he sees himself reflected in the water he transfers to his own image the love that he felt for his dead twin."[32] But Caddy is no dead twin. Quite the opposite: she is more alive than Quentin is. His development is arrested at a childish stage; hers is not—and he knows it. He sees her more as his opposite than as his twin and realizes that he is losing and cannot regain their childhood unity. Such troubles with what looks like imagery arise because Irwin's design draws on Freud's notions of condensation, distortion, and substitution. The design presupposes a "hidden story" that we can "decipher" by condensing and distorting materials in the two novels and by substituting one material for another. If the design allows us to condense, distort, and substitute, what does it prevent us from doing? Are any operations illegitimate? To know what they might be isn't easy. Irwin's design allows him to do what he will with the books and to discover in the gap whatever connections those operations reveal or create. Because of his design Irwin does not comment on the novels themselves, on the novels that Faulkner wrote one at a time or on the novels that are read by people who can choose to read either novel by itself or both in either order. Instead, what Irwin regards as the continuing story hidden in the space between

31. Irwin, 50 and 28.

32. Ibid., 41.

the novels is, I suspect, what Faulkner might have written if he had been a post-Freudian Balzac.

Allusion as Design

Many a reader has noticed that *Absalom* alludes to other works. Cleanth Brooks has discussed its allusions to *Moby-Dick;* Lind, to Greek tragedies; Constance Hill Hall, to Milton; and Irwin, to Robinson Jeffers's "Tamar";[33] but all those critics have wisely refrained from making the allusions the book's determining designs. Yet its very title invites readers to take a biblical allusion as the design. Accepting that invitation, however, has resulted in narrow, rigid interpretations. Even the richest of them, that of Ralph Behrens, cannot encompass the book's complexity. Finding the story of David in 2 Samuel parallel to *Absalom,* Behrens analyzes "four possible theories to account for the failure of Sutpen's design," a design that Behrens defines as "Sutpen's plans for establishing a plantation and founding an aristocratic family, a dynasty." The theories, Behrens adds, "are not mutually exclusive and may even lend support to one another, but the title of the novel . . . constitutes a strong indication that Faulkner expected his readers to find significance in the parallels between his story and the account of the House of David." Behrens's theories propose that (1) Sutpen failed because of his innocence; (2) Sutpen failed because of hubris; (3) Sutpen failed because he tried to emulate the corrupt society of the antebellum South; (4) Sutpen's "failure may be equated with the failure of dynasties of ancient times illustrated in the prophetic books of the Old Testament, where failure appears to lie in the dynastic concept itself." Behrens presents and criticizes the first three theories and offers extensive "analogies between circumstances and events" in the novel and the Bible. He rejects none of the theories, but he finds the first two "narrow . . . because they concentrate on the downfall of a single man." The third appeals more to him because it is "broader"; yet it is "limited by regional and temporal analogy." He prefers his fourth theory that, like the vision of an Old Testament prophet, finds dynasties inherently doomed to fail. "To see the mythic import of the story in relation

33. Cleanth Brooks, *William Faulkner: Toward Yoknapatawpha,* 296; Lind, 278–80 and 287; Hall, 78–88; Irwin, 17–20.

to the Old Testament . . . is to lend universal and timeless significance to Sutpen's story."[34]

Behrens is no doubt right in pointing out how the allusion to
the story of David helps enrich the meaning of *Absalom*. Yet once
the allusion becomes *the* design, it screens out everything in the
novel that has no parallel in the Bible. Much of what distinguishes
the 471-page novel from the 30 pages of 2 Samuel will consequently get filtered out of the interpretation. In particular, although Behrens wants to explain why Sutpen's design failed, he
never comprehends the design at all: it has no analogy in the Bible.
Beyond that, I suspect, difficulties that result from this allusion
derive from the desire for "universal and timeless significance," a
desire that will slay the particular on the altar of the general.

The Representation of History as Design

Of all the designs for bringing *Absalom* within our modes of order,
the most common is to see it as representing or allegorizing history. Eric J. Sundquist proposes a particularly concrete parallel
when he tries to show

> an analogy between Lincoln and Sutpen, each of whom
> labors heroically to build or preserve a magnificent
> "house" symbolic of his national and personal dream, and
> both of whom, at about the same time, face a crisis in the
> house and try desperately to postpone it. In each case, the
> Civil War itself forces a resolution of the crisis—though
> not in either case without violent consequences. It is not
> by any means an analogy in which they or their designs
> are exactly duplicated but, rather, one in which they are
> mirror images in the sense that a mirror image reverses the
> figure to which it corresponds.[35]

One detail of that passage tellingly reveals a design compelling
readers to twist what they have read. The war does not force a
resolution of the Sutpens' crisis: according to *Absalom*, the war
postpones it.

Yet in developing his analogy, Sundquist is uncommonly

34. Behrens, 24, 32 n. 1, 24, 29, 31.

35. Sundquist, 105.

aware of what presuppositions he holds and aware that other critics have held other ones. Objecting to formalism as the "predominant mode in Faulkner criticism," he says that he will reconstruct "a context for Faulkner's fiction out of historical experience, contemporary literature, or political and sociological documents."[36] Sundquist aims to counter the formalists' failure or refusal to attend to a work's cultural context and their failure or refusal to see how cultural contexts inevitably creep into their interpretations anyway.

To construct the context, Sundquist gives blocks of historical and literary background—Stowe's *Dred,* W. J. Cash, *Benito Cereno,* Lincoln's career, the coining of the word *miscegenation,* and the role of the idea of racial mixing in the 1850s and after. But culture doesn't manifest itself as blocks plunked down in a work. Culture permeates every pore of the work and manifests itself at every level: word choice, sentence structure, act, ritual, history, genre, and so on. To interpret *Absalom* in its cultural context is essential, but Sundquist's method lacks the delicacy and precision that cultural interpretation requires.

Sundquist is right, however, in calling much Faulkner criticism formalist. But if *formalist* implies close reading, the critics, including Sundquist, haven't read closely enough. Sutpen's design has escaped him, too. His analogy to Lincoln leads him to see Sutpen's and Lincoln's aims as analogous mirror images:

> We do not, I think, have to torture Lincoln's position too much to make it resemble Sutpen's dilemma over the recognition of his "black" son, Charles Bon: if Lincoln had let the abolition of slavery take its own eventual course, his restoration of the Union would indeed, to some observers then and perhaps to all in retrospect, have been "a mockery and a betrayal"; by abolishing slavery "with [his] own hand," he necessarily destroyed the design—for saving the Union without interfering with slavery where it already existed—that he had insisted on time and again. Lincoln was ready to assume the role of the founding fathers and preserve their design . . . but he was often . . . paternalistic . . . toward blacks. . . . Likewise, Thomas Sutpen is determined to continue to enhance the Southern design of a

36. Ibid., x.

slaveholding paternalism, but he is not ready to accept a "Negro" son into that design.[37]

The racial question was Lincoln's crisis; Sundquist's analogy therefore makes him exaggerate its role in Sutpen's story. Sutpen is in a dilemma over recognizing Bon, not because Bon is black but because he is not a nameless stranger. Sundquist also errs in assuming that Sutpen wants "to continue to enhance" the southern plantation culture; his design is to construct a rifle to fire at it. While I won't guess what Sutpen would have done if a *black* nameless stranger had knocked at his door, opening the door to him would not have violated Sutpen's design. Opening the door to his own son, white or black, would have.

The history that readers most often want to make *Absalom* represent is the history of the South. Lyall H. Powers, for example, points to that design as if it were unquestionable: "The parallels between Sutpen's career specifically and the history of the South generally are obvious; his career is a microcosmic emblem of the Southern macrocosm. Understanding of Sutpen yields understanding of the South, for Quentin and for us."[38]

Presenting a more elaborate but similar argument, Daniel Joseph Singal interprets Judith, Henry, and Bon on what he calls an "almost allegorical level, as representations of the three main forms of social order in the South, the frontier, the town, and the Tidewater" or as representations of "backwoods vitality, small-town probity, and Cavalier identity." "On the level of social allegory," Singal says, the Sutpen children's "incest triangle appears to indicate Faulkner's belief that the predominant social institutions of the Old South failed to reach maturity." From the children's being so drawn to one another, Singal concludes that "neither Tidewater, small town, nor frontier has, in this allegory, developed the values and inner coherence necessary to exist by itself as a viable form of social organization." The children thus constitute, on the one hand, "a refutation, almost a parody, of the familiar conception of the South as a stable, well-structured organic society." On the other hand, they also refute W. J. Cash's "opposing notion of the Old South as . . . an 'aggregation of self-contained and self-sufficient monads.'" For Singal, then, "Sutpen

37. Ibid., 106–7.
38. Powers, 110.

represents the total negation of the mythical Cavalier. He is the planter as nouveau riche, the southern aristocrat as self-made man, whose every action hinges on his self-centered, calculating ambition." Faulkner makes his attack on the Cavalier ironic by rooting Sutpen's materialism not in greed but in innocence. "If a curse did lie on the South, then, one could trace its origin not to slavery or racial segregation—important though these were—but to this trait of stubborn, pervasive, disabling innocence that arose through the frontier character of southern society and caused southerners to adopt identities hopelessly inauthentic, based on mythology rather than on actual historical roots."[39] Simple or elaborate, every version of the design that takes *Absalom* as representing southern history must fail for the same reason. We don't read about Sutpen's design before page 260. But if, by then, a reader believes that the book's movement will parallel southern history, then the reader is unlikely to be able to grasp Sutpen's design. His design is to attack the southern social structure in a way that certainly had no historical parallel. To open the door to the nameless stranger directly opposes the principles of the southern culture that these readers want the book to parallel. Their design has blinded them to what the book actually says.

Francis Garvin Davenport, Jr., extends Sutpen's symbolic reach by making him the "Southerner as American." Here, again, a historical parallel proves blinding. In saying that Sutpen created his design "for the sake of revenge, and supposedly in order to be able himself to meet the poor white boy next time and to admit him into the great house," Davenport comes close to grasping the design, even though he qualifies his description with the *supposedly.* Even so, Davenport then simply dismisses the design as no more than "the American dream of success."[40]

Cleanth Brooks also regards Sutpen as being more representative of Americans than just of the southern planter class. Citing evidence from Eugene Genovese and C. Vann Woodward, Brooks contends instead that Sutpen is a representative American within the Protestant ethic.[41] Brooks's view here seems sounder than his opponents' views do: Sutpen's mountain egalitarianism is quintessentially American and Protestant, not simply southern.

39. Singal, 190–92, 193, 188, 189, 190.

40. Davenport, 97, 98, 99.

41. Cleanth Brooks, *William Faulkner: Toward Yoknapatawpha,* 283–300.

Nevertheless, Brooks misunderstands Sutpen's design. Brooks considers him as drawing from the Protestant ethic his asceticism, rationalism, and obsessiveness. Yet Sutpen's design carries egalitarianism well beyond American norms. America has opened its door to nameless strangers; but, the Statue of Liberty notwithstanding, the American motive for doing so was not Sutpen's. His motives were both vindictive and high-minded. He sought to defend the little boy by striking a blow at the southern patriarchy or perhaps at patriarchy generally, and he intended to free the nameless stranger from brutehood. The American door-opening was pragmatic: the country needed more people. And Americans saw no need to separate these strangers from brutehood; for blacks to serve as slaves, for the Chinese and the Irish to die by the thousands in building railroads and tunnels, or for eastern Europeans to live in slums and starve on piecework wages was, by and large, quite acceptable.

Thus, Brooks's design, in which *Absalom* represents American history, misleads him just as others were misled by taking the book as an emblem or allegory of the South. These designs quickly draw readers so far away from the book that they fail to notice details that are crucial to understanding what it means. To deny that *Absalom* represents southern or American history does not, of course, set it in a never-never land isolated from history and culture. Faulkner remains a Mississippian, a southerner, and an American writing in the 1930s and drawing on the history and culture he knows best. As a result they are the materials with which *Absalom* constructs its physical, historical, and cultural setting and its characters' cultural assumptions and motives. Knowing a good deal about the South is therefore probably essential to understanding the book, even though *Absalom* does not aim to represent or to allegorize the processes of southern or American history.

Lack of Design as Design

When hypotheses about workable designs keep failing, a reader may feel frustrated. "Discovering a design is impossible," such a reader may conclude, only to say, "Aha, *that's* the design—'designs are impossible'!" James Guetti takes a position like that: "The inability of the narrators to understand the experience surrounding Sutpen may be an expression of a consistent theme: that human experience cannot be understood, that order cannot be created." One might dismiss Guetti's hypothesis as self-contradictory since a work that denies the creation of order must have created order to convey the denial. Instead, let's see where Guetti goes with his hypothesis. Guetti is using *Absalom,* along with *Moby-Dick* and "Heart of Darkness," to show how the "formal disintegration in the novel" derives from the "disparity between language in general and something that appears to be inexpressible, which we might call 'life' or 'truth' or 'reality.'" That disintegration occurs when "the fundamental imaginative process of creating, discarding, and re-creating order . . . accelerates" and "the imagination is called upon more and more frequently to create, by manipulating the diversities of its perceptions, new and stable order." Imagination then grows incapable of conceiving a "reality" that it can find real, and language consequently cannot express this "ineffable" reality, as Guetti calls it.[42]

Yet despite his design, which is assuring him that human experience may finally be incomprehensible, Guetti comes remarkably close to comprehending Sutpen's own design. Guetti sees that Sutpen aims at more than founding a dynasty and even at more than combating the Tidewater planter's class. Sutpen intends to "combat . . . the rules by which the class is established. He will combat these rules by means of the possessions that express the rules. . . . he is attempting to make use of the social system to overcome that system." Having comprehended that much, Guetti then strays from the mark: "By entering the house, Sutpen will be enabled to transform himself and his descendants. They are to . . . have—like Sutpen himself—a meaningful identity." Guetti goes on to say that "this identity is finally based on the acquiring of possessions. . . . for Sutpen the void of his life is to be filled with possessions and descendants, which in turn must be expressive of a completely controlled and defined design."[43]

How could Guetti have gotten so close and still not have felt the force of Sutpen's desire to open the door to the nameless stranger? That question suggests another. Although Guetti notices the third-person narration, he writes, "Quentin is the sum of all the narrators," and "the anonymous narrator . . . refuses to sanction the entire narrative as anything more than hypothesis." Why couldn't Guetti feel the third-person narrator's power? The an-

42. Guetti, 69–70, 1, 2, 3.

43. Ibid., 84–85.

swer, I think, is that if reality must be ineffable, if "human experience cannot be understood," and if "order cannot be created," then Sutpen's design, his vision of the world that he wants to bring into being, would inevitably be as Guetti finds it: "a void, a nothingness." Guetti's design precludes his understanding Sutpen's and compels Guetti into untenable positions. He says, for example, that Sutpen's "refusal to recognize Bon in any way seems insane, out of all proportion to what we suppose are the facts." And he says that "what is truly inexplicable here is that Bon seems to pose no literal threat whatever to the design." If the narrators were to tell the story so as to convey a convincing "reality," then *Absalom* would no longer fit Guetti's design. As long as the enigma endures, he can assert that "it is no longer a question of Mr. Compson's errors or Rosa's ignorance: there can be no errors or ignorance in a narrative world where we are concerned with what cannot be meaningful or what may not exist as comprehensible experience at all." Guetti says that whatever Mr. Compson "cannot explain he characteristically redefines as what cannot be explained."[44] So, it may seem, does Guetti.

If Guetti were right, would anyone then want to reread *Absalom* after having discovered that trying to understand it is an exercise in futility? Christine de Montauzon thinks that we enjoy the exercise. She argues that "*Absalom* . . . is marked by a permanent non-fulfillment of all the elicited and often contradictory codes through an absence of sufficient support from the text. As an 'open work' *Absalom* offers a vast testing field of potential meanings, all of which ultimately abort in the maze of the text itself." No matter how "open" a work may be, its meaning cannot be entirely open. All the interpretive codes from syntax to genre conspire to limit openness. Utter openness would be equivalent to meaninglessness. Committed to keeping the work open, Montauzon never even asks what Sutpen's design is. She does recognize the voice of the third-person narrator in the scene in which Henry goes to Sutpen's tent. The narrator, she says, there becomes "one with Quentin-Shreve / Henry-Bon. He knows what they know but is also ignorant of what they do not know." Such a narrator would, of course, be unreliable: "The implied author remains ambiguously mixed up with the other points of view and confused with their restricted scope as characters. Hence structure as a point

44. Ibid., 103, 93, 87, 88, 80, 70.

of view lacks a center in *Absalom*."[45] While preventing Montauzon from seeing the closure that exists, her resistance protects her from closing an interpretation prematurely. As a result her interpretations are subtle, and her critiques of the interpretations of others are astute and just.

The Process of Historical Analysis as Design

A number of critics have argued that *Absalom* is seeking the nature of history and testing its limits. As Waggoner says:

> Quentin's effort to understand Sutpen is an attempt to interpret all history. . . . Quentin encounters two conflicting modes of interpretation [Rosa's and Mr. Compson's], is satisfied by neither, and creates, with Shreve, a third. . . .
> . . . history contains both God's judgment and man's decision, both necessity and freedom, and it has sufficient intelligibility for our human purposes. But its meaning is neither given nor entirely withheld. It must be achieved, created by imagination and faith. Historical meaning is a construct.[46]

A few years later Cleanth Brooks reached the same conclusion—that " 'history' is really a kind of imaginative construction"—through a slightly more developed rationale: "The novel . . . has to do not merely with the meaning of Sutpen's career but with the nature of historical truth and with the problem of how we can 'know' the past. The importance of this . . . theme determines the very special way in which the story of Sutpen is mediated to us through a series of partial disclosures, informed guesses, and constantly revised deductions and hypotheses."[47]

As a design for *Absalom,* historical analysis presents a hazard of its own. The historian must rely on witnesses and documents. These can report and record people's acts and words, but people's motives always remain hidden. Historians cannot look into the mind or the heart. Even people who offer ostensible explanations of their own motives are unreliable witnesses: our own minds and hearts may be closed to us. All that being so, the reader who takes

45. Montauzon, xv, 255, 257.

46. Waggoner, *William Faulkner: From Jefferson,* 167 and 168.

47. Cleanth Brooks, *William Faulkner: Yoknapatawpha Country,* 311 and 309.

historical analysis as the design cannot trust any narrator's account; it cannot be more reliable than a historian's. The reader cannot trust even the "he said" of a third-person narrator. In works of fiction, that conventional phrase makes the speaker's having said certain words a fact. In history there are no third-person narrators, and so Waggoner can hear "no official, sanctioned Voice" in *Absalom*.[48] So, too, Brooks feels that he must caution us that "it is worth remarking that we do not 'know,' apart from the Quentin-Shreve semifictional process, many events which a casual reader assumes actually happened."[49]

Neither Brooks nor Waggoner makes historical analysis the book's only design. Both of them regard tragedy, a design that we will examine shortly, as at least equally important. I share that interest in both historical analysis and tragedy but regard them as subordinate designs. More needs to be said here, though, about how historical analysis and fiction fit together. Carl E. Rollyson, Jr., surveys the boundary that history cannot pass. Quoting the historian Herbert Butterfield, Rollyson says that "history as the historian writes it 'cannot come so near to human hearts and human passions as a good novel can; its very fidelity to facts makes it not perhaps less true to life, but farther away from the heart of things.'" Therefore, he examines *Absalom* to see how far its "historical" analysis can penetrate into the heart of things and where the techniques of fiction must take over.[50]

Sutpen's design eludes him. "Bon's Negro blood," he writes, "is the 'factor' which Sutpen could not privately accept, even though, as he says to General Compson, in the eyes of the public his design would have been complete once (we can infer) Bon had married Judith." Not seeing Sutpen's design as problematic, Rollyson concentrates on trying to understand how Quentin and Shreve work as historians. Rollyson's interest in historical analysis as a design does not, however, keep him from noticing the third-person narrator. Even so, Rollyson treats the account of Henry's meeting Sutpen in his tent as Quentin's and Shreve's creation as historians, not as the narrator's account: "In truth, this passage is essentially an extension and heightening of what Quentin and Shreve have already been imagining as Henry's viewpoint." While

48. Waggoner, *William Faulkner: From Jefferson*, 148.

49. Cleanth Brooks, *William Faulkner: Yoknapatawpha Country*, 312.

50. Rollyson, *Uses of the Past*, 92.

that view is, I think, wrong, his overall judgment seems correct. There is, he concludes, "no third-person narrator who can confidently summarize the meaning of the narratives as totalities." Nonetheless, Rollyson says, although the scene in Sutpen's tent stems from "the emotional as well as the intellectual transactions of Quentin and Shreve," it goes well beyond what they can know as historians and attains "an achieved imaginative whole": "the actual experience of hearing and seeing Sutpen, Henry, and Bon speak to each other." Rollyson's argument thus gives weight both to historical analysis and to fiction. And since *Absalom* also requires us to weigh them both ourselves, he can say, "Not only do Quentin and Shreve succeed as narrators because they have learned to think historically, but also our awareness of history gradually expands as we learn to assess their use of historical method and their attempts to go beyond it."[51] Rollyson's interpretation is therefore valuable for showing how *Absalom* uses historical analysis to its limit and then turns to fiction to pierce to the heart of things.

Narrative Form as Design

Joseph W. Reed, Jr., elevates these distinctions between kinds of narrative from questions of stylistic tactics to the book's very subject. "To begin to understand *Absalom, Absalom!*," he says, "is . . . to move beyond what may seem to be the centers of the book—a hero, a story, a dream, a myth, a tragedy—into the process of narrative itself by which these apparent centers are revealed. . . . Could not telling and hearing themselves be at the heart of the book?" His answer, of course, is yes: *Absalom* "is a narrative about narrative."[52]

From that premise Reed argues that one cannot attain and so should not seek "a deep understanding of Thomas Sutpen." Reed's concern for how the story gets told deafens him to what gets told: he does not understand Sutpen's design. And, oddly for a book on narrative, he seems at times to go astray in his comments on the narrators. He calls "Quentin the Teller and Shreve the Hearer." In saying that they seek "a perfect arrangement" of the narrative and most basically want "to make it work," Reed overlooks the fact that they are interested less in the whole Sutpen story than in the

51. Ibid., 61, 57–58, 71, 93, 97.

52. Reed, 146 and 147.

story of Bon, Judith, and Henry. Finally Reed does little with what he calls "the narrative presence"—that is, the third-person narrator.[53] Nevertheless, Reed seems correct in calling for readers to attend to narrative itself as a design for *Absalom*.

The designs that a good many readers have found in it stem from their having adopted, consciously or not, Shreve's romantic design, Rosa's Gothic design, or Mr. Compson's tragic one and having extended it to the whole book. Some toy, at least, with adopting as their design Shreve's wish for a narrative quest-romance better than *Ben Hur*. Reed sees *Absalom* as partly a "puzzle" and a "whodunit," and Cleanth Brooks calls it "from one point of view a wonderful detective story."[54] According to Schoenberg, the "Sutpen stories" are "a body of tales told by a collection of raconteurs" and "a series of dramatically potent pictures, irresistible to imaginations born and bred to spin yarns."[55] Her words come close to describing *Absalom* as the narrative romance in its simplest form, the vivid string of adventures in folktales and comic strips. But in the end no one, not even Shreve, sees the quest-romance as the book's design. *Absalom*'s outcomes are too grim and its tone is too dark for that.

Rosa's narrative stance, however, has dominated some interpretations. They take two forms. The more common resists Rosa's narrative vision by launching an all-out counterattack. A passage from Vickery, for instance, will suggest that approach: "Though Miss Rosa knew Sutpen most intimately, her account of him is the most distorted, revealing only her own obsession, the narrowness of her experience, and the grim inflexibility of her responses. . . . Miss Rosa's account of Sutpen and of the past in general is rank melodrama and . . . all the characters in it are exaggerated, distorted phantoms."[56] If that view were adequate, it might go so far as to imply that omitting Rosa's narrative would have improved the book. In fact, we learn from Rosa a considerable amount about Judith and Clytie and about Sutpen after his return from the war; and those observations, at least, seem perceptive and seldom biased. To counter Rosa's view, Vickery

53. Ibid., 150, 168, 169, 173.

54. Ibid., 145 and 146; Cleanth Brooks, *William Faulkner: Yoknapatawpha Country*, 311.

55. Schoenberg, 134 and 135.

56. Vickery, 87–88.

chooses a design, "rank melodrama," that is itself an exaggerated, distorted phantom rather than an accurate term for Rosa's chapters.

The less common approach, and the worse distortion, accepts Rosa's view and reads the rest of the book through it. A couple of sentences from Kerr can represent that kind of reading: "Miss Rosa's impassioned style and her demonizing created the Gothic tone and the character of Sutpen. . . . The other narrators echoed Rosa's tone with variations and added their own interpretations to hers."[57] Kerr is partly right: Rosa's style and demonizing do set a Gothic tone, but only in the opening. Rosa's first chapter, however, conveys little of Sutpen's character. In the next three chapters, some 130 pages, Mr. Compson covers Sutpen's whole career in Jefferson so that by the time we reach Rosa's other chapter—which is more reportorial and less Gothic—our new information reveals Rosa's prejudices. We can see her demonizing as melodramatic. Those still blinded by it ought to have their eyes opened during the following chapters, in which Quentin reports Sutpen's conversations with General Compson and in which Shreve caricatures Rosa and keeps repeating with heavy irony her word *demon*. The other characters, then, undermine her tone rather than echoing it and revise her portrait of Sutpen by altering rather than merely adding to it. However, once Kerr has taken Rosa's Gothic narrative as her own design, it conceals from her more than it reveals.

The Gothic also dominates Irving Howe's vision of *Absalom*. Yet Howe is less single-minded than Vickery and Kerr are on the subject of the Gothic. He sees Sutpen as partly standing for the South: "Sartoris and Sutpen seem to equal . . . traditional Southern character. . . . Just because Sutpen is not a 'typical' Southern plantation owner, he expresses with terrible nakedness a central quality of the traditional South." Consequently, Howe feels that he can apply to Sutpen the judgment that Mr. Compson attributes to Mr. Coldfield. Howe says, "In defeat, the South, like Sutpen himself, 'was paying the price for having erected its economic edifice not on the rock of stern morality but on the shifting sands of opportunism and moral brigandage.' Moral brigandage—that should be plain enough."[58] "Opportunism," even if it fits the

57. Kerr, *William Faulkner's Gothic Domain,* 46.

58. Howe, 74, and 78.

South, seems to misrepresent Sutpen. He hasn't lucked into op-
portunities but has struggled to create them, and he has constantly
acted in accordance with the principle of his design. "Moral brigandage" may be apt for describing slaveholding, but it is hardly
"plain enough" for describing Sutpen. The noun implies banditry,
as if Sutpen had stolen that steamboat; and the adjective fails to
clarify Howe's meaning. Does it suggest that Sutpen has robbed
people of their morals? That he is a brigand but a moral one? By
dragging in Mr. Coldfield's words, Howe makes it necessary to
explain, or explain away, their implications but doesn't do so. The
edifice that Sutpen sought to erect was not simply economic; he
meant to shelter the nameless stranger. And if the edifice was not
to be erected on the rock of stern morality, still Sutpen's desire to
open the door—thereby freeing the stranger and his descendants
from brutehood forever and firing a shot designed to pierce the
armor of dynastic society—strikes me as a moral aim. What Howe
probably wanted to say was merely that Sutpen acted immorally.
His means were wrong; his end, however, was not. The phrase
"opportunism and moral brigandage" is self-righteous and imprecise. With it Howe cannot express the distinctions necessary to
understand Sutpen's design.

Although noticing that Sutpen "closely approximates the
tragic hero," Howe finally charges him with not only opportunism and moral brigandage but also a "failure in self-recognition"
and defines him as no more than "a satanic hero." Thus for Howe
"the Gothic is qualified as the story moves toward narrators de-
creasingly involved with its protagonists, but the effects of Gothic
linger to the end."[59]

Although Howe takes Sutpen's question about where he
made the mistake in his design as "the central question of the
book," Howe sees the design merely as founding a large, luxuri-
ous plantation and owning and dominating men.[60] Howe's assumption that the Gothic colors everything in *Absalom* may make
that misreading inevitable and preclude his understanding Sutpen's design. Although representative figures and tragic heroes
may conventionally have noble or naive aims, Gothic heroes cannot; their aims must be egocentric or evil.

The Gothic, while not dominant in *Absalom,* is of course

59. Ibid., 74–75, 223, 72.
60. Ibid., 75–77.

strong and deserves, as Max Putzel has said, to be given "no more than its due." He finds the Gothic in images recalling medieval chivalry, images that "identify Sutpen with the chivalric culture he has tried to emulate," in "Rosa's idea of Sutpen as demonic knight and satanic upstart," and in "allusions to ancient French style and manner—to Bayard and Carcassonne." Refusing to overstate the power of the Gothic, Putzel judges—rightly, I think—that the tragic is stronger; indeed, many readers have found the book fundamentally tragic. Richard Sewall says, "The total vision is neither of doom nor redemption, but of something tantalizingly, precariously in between. We have no hope, yet we hope. It is tragic." And Lind says that "the intention of *Absalom, Absalom!* is to create . . . a grand tragic vision of historic dimension."[61]

Yet readers who consider the novel tragic may disagree about whose tragedy it is. Sewall says that Sutpen has "some of the qualities and many of the trappings of a tragic hero." But if he undergoes the hero's spiritual ordeal, it "is only hinted at and its results never articulated. It is not that Sutpen had 'forgotten the infinite'; he never knew it. . . . His fall, like Agamemnon's, was moral, not tragic." Sewall comes close to Sutpen's design by the simple expedient of quoting, without comment, the most relevant of the words in which Sutpen describes his design. Even so, those words and the situation in which they are uttered—Sutpen's need to go to General Compson's office to say them to him—do not induce Sewall to infer that Sutpen is undergoing a spiritual ordeal. "The tragedy is Quentin's," Sewall concludes, although *Absalom* takes Quentin only through what Sewall calls the initiation, the first stage of the tragic narrative pattern. "The truth of Sutpen's story . . . is the source of its terror for Quentin, the glimpse it gives him into the abyss."[62]

To Cleanth Brooks, on the other hand, the tragedy is Sutpen's: Sutpen "achieves a kind of grandeur. Even the obsessed Miss Rosa sees him as great, not as petty and sordid. His innocence resembles that of Oedipus (who, like him, had been corrupted by success and who put his confidence in his own shrewdness). His courage resembles that of Macbeth, and like Macbeth he is 'resolute to try the last.' Perhaps the most praise-

61. Putzel, 5, 10, 13; Sewall, 147; Lind, 278.

62. Sewall, 138, 142–43, 143, 147.

worthy aspect of Faulkner is his ability to create a character of heroic proportions and to invest his downfall with something like tragic dignity."[63]

Waggoner considers *Absalom* a divided tragedy with the story of the Sutpens as the tragic action and with Quentin's and Shreve's viewpoint as the tragic vision. Waggoner describes their judgment on "Sutpen's *hubris,* his narrow rationalism, his lack of love" as deriving from their understanding his story as "classical-Christian tragedy."[64] Lind agrees that the tragedy is divided but says:

> The narrators themselves, lost in their private obsessions and viewing the Sutpen story only partially through their individual distortions of vision, do not see the meaning of the tragedy in which they play a part nor its relation to the one they have made. Only the reader has a full view of the stage. He sees, as it were, two tragedies on a single theme, simultaneously enacted. The curtain lifts on a play within a play: on the inner stage, the Sutpen drama; on the outer, the larger social tragedy involving the narrators. The second creates the first, and the first serves to convey the second.[65]

Lynn Gartrell Levins proposes adopting all of the four narrators' forms: Rosa's Gothic, Mr. Compson's Greek tragedy, Quentin's chivalric romance, and Shreve's talltale. If we follow that advice, she says, "the result is that not one figure of Thomas Sutpen emerges by the end of the novel, but four."[66] Their emergence would, I think, imply a misreading: the book's effect is more unified than that. *Absalom* hardly puts the talltale to the test; Shreve's model is *Ben Hur* rather than Paul Bunyan. The Gothic and the chivalric romance fail under the pressures of the narrative: they cannot account for enough. Three of Levins's four forms do not stand on equal footing with tragedy.

Obviously, none of the critics attempting to define the book's narrative form was likely to succeed because none understood its

63. Cleanth Brooks, *William Faulkner: Yoknapatawpha Country,* 307.

64. Waggoner, 167.

65. Lind, 286.

66. Levins, 9.

narrative. They did not see what we now know: that Sutpen aimed to open the door and, by doing so, to strike at southern culture. His opening the door would have not only astonished his fellow southerners but also exemplified some principles of a finer morality than those of the Tidewater South or of his own mountain culture.

Moral purists will object that his aim, however noble, cannot justify his means. That's so. Yet weighing the main character's virtues against his vices so as to decide whether he got what he deserved seems as far from the mark in *Absalom* as in *Oedipus Rex* and *King Lear*. Like Oedipus, Sutpen exists in a world constructed to thwart his best impulse. As Oedipus' world is designed so that his flight takes him to the fate he is fleeing, so in Sutpen's world "while he was still playing the scene to the audience, behind him Fate, destiny, retribution, irony—the stage manager, call him what you will" (87–88)—was bringing to his door Charles Bon, whose knock confronts Sutpen with the dilemma we have examined. The world in which Sutpen acts seems to lie between the boundaries that *King Lear* surveys, between "As flies to wanton boys, are we to the gods, / They kill us for their sport" (4.1.37–38) and "The gods are just, and of our pleasant vices / Make instruments to plague us" (5.3.170–71). When we grasp his design and all its implications and consequences, we discover in Sutpen what is rare in modern literature: a tragic hero.

Epilogue on Reading as Designing

The designs that readers have used have mostly led them to misunderstand *Absalom*—hardly a cheering prospect for us as readers ourselves. Yet our findings as we have surveyed the criticism imply, at least, some ways to avoid similar misreadings.

We began to seek the meaning of a literary text with the act by which readers make texts into literature. John M. Ellis has described that act:

> When . . . we treat a piece of language as literature, we characteristically do something quite surprising: we no longer accept any information offered as something to act upon, nor do we act on its exhortations and imperatives. We do not generally concern ourselves with whether what it says is true or false, or regard it as relevant to any specific practical purpose. In sum, we no longer respond to it as

part of the immediate context we live in and as something to use in our normal way as a means of controlling that context; nor do we concern ourselves with the immediate context from which it emerged, and so are not taking it up to learn, in our normal way, something about that actual everyday context. Assertions about literature similar to these may well, in themselves, be familiar; but what is here of the utmost importance is that they are not simply true statements about literature, but constitute the *definition* of literature.

When readers choose to treat a text as not "specifically relevant to the immediate context of its origin," the text becomes, for them, literature.[67] Readers, and groups of readers, are free to choose to treat as literature whatever texts they wish. Writers' intentions don't govern their choices. Works that writers offer as literature may not be accepted, and readers may treat as literature a work— for instance, a letter—whose writer did not intend it to be literature.

After choosing to treat a text as literature, the reader takes the steps that are entailed by the culture's conception of the act of reading literature. In this culture those steps would include assuming that the text should not be changed once its authenticity has been established, assuming that the text is complete in itself, assuming that any detail is likely to be significant, paying close attention to the text, and assuming that the text is rereadable and not easily exhaustible.

At this point interpretation begins. In reading we try to naturalize the text by finding in it—or, more accurately, by giving it—a design, by relating it to some other model that seems familiar and therefore natural. Kenneth Burke has sketched a way to break down our interpretive process into its elements. He imagines, first, that we construct a concordance to bring together the "facts" of similar words recurring in changing contexts throughout the text. Next, "we must find some principle of selection, since some terms are much more likely than others to yield good hermeneutical results." These words he calls key terms, words that recur often and seem important because of what they refer to or because they connect to many other terms. But "where do we start? Where do we stop?" he asks. "Let us admit: there must be a

67. Ellis, 43–44.

certain amount of waste motion here. . . . anything might pay off.
. . . And we must keep on the move, watching both for static
interrelationships and for principles of transformation whereby a
motive may progress from one combination through another to a
third."[68]

While putting together our concordance, trying out key
terms, and watching for terms to transmute themselves, Burke
says, we look for "stages" and "sub-stages" by trying to answer
the question "Suppose you were required to find an overall title
for this entire batch of particulars. What would that be?" We note
oppositions, appositions, beginnings and endings, transitions and
breaks, names, properties present in more than one character, internal forms, "a point of farthest internality," details of scene, and
first appearances. We look for "expressions marking secrecy, privacy, mystery, marvel, power, silence, guilt. Such terms are likely
to point in the direction of central concerns in all cultures." We
also look for the text's views of society's tensions and for the text's
synonyms for *order;* they will imply a social structure. We look for
"a symbolic solution"—a catharsis or a transcendence—and for
ironic reversals. We look, too, for moments when "the work
comes to fruition." "One proceeds from such places, where the
work comes to a temporary head. One radiates in search of laby-
rinthine internal consistency, while at the same time watching for
progressions. One tries to be aware of one's shifts between 'fac-
tuality' and 'thematic' generalizing. One watches for overall social
tensions, and for the varying tactics of 'purification' with regard
to them. And one is thereby talking about 'symbolism,' willy-
nilly."[69]

By this slow detailing of steps, Burke is trying to counter a
tendency that we have seen in most critics writing on *Absalom,* the
tendency to jump too quickly to designs and to land on oversim-
ple ones at that. Burke explains in part why we often succumb to
the temptation to jump: "The 'analogical' method is alluring, because by it you get these things settled once and for all. A good
literature student, trained in the ways of 'analogizing,' can depart
from the text at the drop of a hat, whereas the indexing of 'contexts' requires that each work be studied anew, 'from scratch.'
Night, bird, sun, blood, tree, mountain, death? No matter, once

68. Burke, 287–88, 290 (italics omitted).

69. Ibid., 290, 296–99 (italics omitted), 300, 301, 306.

the topic is introduced, analogy has the answer, without ever looking further."[70] Burke thus places the blame for faulty reading mainly on laziness. He may, however, be too harsh a judge. Perhaps *Absalom* so strains one's powers to recall details, to judge conflicting accounts, and even to comprehend syntax that no one who has read it several times can justly be called lazy. Nevertheless, one might wish that its critics had paid it closer attention.

I see another culprit as well. To interpret literature calls for us to test and to tentatively reject and accept hypothetical designs. As a result, reading keeps us immersed in uncertainty. Yet we may not welcome, may not even tolerate, uncertainty that is either intense or long-lasting; the uncertainty in *Absalom* is both. Under those conditions readers are tempted to clutch whatever interpretive design lies near at hand, declaring by fiat which details are crucial and which are not. Having chosen designs, the readers have fewer things to keep in mind and to try to account for. Yearning for certainty, they therefore rush to some design—a critical theory, the Faulkner canon, an allusion, history, historical analysis, or narrative form—thereby closing themselves off from other important details and useful designs.

Haste in choosing designs also precludes the reader's appreciating the uniqueness of *Absalom*. Much that sets it apart from all other works—particularly the singularity of Sutpen's design—is made invisible. Criticism has distorted *Absalom* by underemphasizing how much its own design differs from those of the models that critics have compared it with. Insufficient attention, the fear of uncertainty, and a consequent haste to find designs to cling to have all contributed to failures to see crucial meanings in *Absalom*.

Of course, some critics are arguing that the question "Exactly what does this work mean?" is naive, old-fashioned, and pointless. They are trying to brush it aside by offering two dismissive answers. Deconstructionists are finding that every text contradicts and so dismantles itself. Reader-response critics, on the other hand, are endowing readers with the power to give the text whatever meaning they wish. But neither of those answers can, I think, succeed in dismissing the question. The deconstructionists' conclusion is as predictable as the conclusion of a drugstore romance and therefore as comforting (and boring). The reader-response critics will accept every reader's notion about a

70. Ibid., 286.

text's meaning so long as the notion is interesting. But as Tzvetan Todorov has asked, "Who would dare require historians to throw all care for truth to the winds and try only to be interesting? Who would accept that 'interest' should be the sole guideline in the discourse of a judge or a politician? But when it comes to the amusement park of literature, no one is dismayed by an irresponsible opinion."[71] The hyperbole of his last sentence is no doubt ironic: the energetic debates that fill the pages of scholarly journals express plenty of dismay, as his own words do.

Some critical theorists, however, are less sanguine than I in expecting deconstruction and reader-response criticism to evaporate like the morning dew. George Steiner, for example, says, "I do not perceive any adequate logical or epistemological refutation of deconstructive semiotics." Still, he says,

> if we wish to . . . meet the challenge of . . . "anti-textuality" on grounds as radical as its own, we must bring to bear on the act of meaning, on the understanding of meaning, the full force of moral intuition. . . .
>
>   I take the ethical inference to . . . make the following *morally,* not logically, not empirically, self-evident. The poem comes before the commentary. The primary text is first not only temporally. It is not a pre-text, an occasion for subsequent exegetic or metamorphic treatment. Its priority is one of essence, of ontological need and self-sufficiency. Even the greatest critique or commentary is dependent, secondary, contingent. The poem embodies and bodies forth through a singular enactment its own *raison d'être.* The secondary text does not contain an imperative of being.[72]

For Steiner that ethical inference alone will not suffice to counter the deconstructionists' "nihilistic supposition." We must make a leap of faith:

> We must read as if the text before us had meaning. . . . the meaning striven towards will never be one which exegesis, commentary, translation, paraphrase, psychoanalytic or sociological decoding, can ever exhaust, can ever define as total. . . . Where we read truly, . . . we do so as if the text

71. Todorov, 1093.

72. Steiner, 1262.

. . . incarnates (the notion is grounded in the sacramental) a real presence of significant being. This real presence, as in an icon, as in the enacted metaphor of the sacramental bread and wine, is, finally, irreducible to any other formal articulation, to any analytic deconstruction or paraphrase. It is a singularity.

Lest we feel that his eloquence has carried him into the empyrean, he assures us that "these are not occult notions. They are of the immensity of the commonplace. They are perfectly pragmatic, experiential, repetitive, each and every time a poem, a passage of prose seizes upon our thoughts and feelings, enters into the sinews of our remembrance and sense of the future."[73]

Most readers, whether they must make Steiner's leap or not, will continue to read in the hope that they can find out exactly what the text means; and they are right, I believe, in doing so. By attending carefully to what *Absalom* says and by following roughly the interpretive process that I have outlined in the last few paragraphs, we have, it seems to me, come closer to understanding *Absalom, Absalom!*

73. Ibid., 1275.

Bibliography

Index

Bibliography

Adamowski, T. H. "Children of the Idea: Heroes and Family Romances in *Absalom, Absalom!*" *Mosaic* 10 (Fall 1976): 115–31. Reprinted in Muhlenfeld, *William Faulkner's* Absalom, 135–55.

———. "Dombey and Son and Sutpen and Son." *Studies in the Novel, North Texas State* 4 (1972): 378–89.

Adams, Richard P. "The Apprenticeship of William Faulkner." In *Faulkner: Four Decades of Criticism.* Edited by Linda Welshimer Wagner. East Lansing: Michigan State Univ. Press, 1973.

———. *Faulkner: Myth and Motion.* Princeton: Princeton Univ. Press, 1968.

———. "Faulkner: The European Roots." In *Faulkner: Fifty Years after* The Marble Faun. Edited by George H. Wolfe. University: Univ. of Alabama Press, 1976.

Allen, Walter. *The Modern Novel in Britain and the United States.* New York: Dutton, 1964.

———. *The Urgent West: The American Dream and the Modern Man.* New York: Dutton, 1969.

Allums, Larry. "Overpassing to Love: Dialogue and Play in *Absalom, Absalom!*" *New Orleans Review* 14 (Winter 1987): 36–41.

Anderson, Charles R. "Faulkner's Moral Center." *Collection des Etudes Anglaises* 7 (Jan. 1954): 48–58.

Angell, Leslie E. "The Umbilical Cord Symbol as Unifying Theme and Pattern in *Absalom, Absalom!*" *Massachusetts Studies in English* 1 (1968): 106–10.

Antrim, Harry T. "Faulkner's Suspended Style." *University of Kansas City Review* 32 (Winter 1965): 122–28.

Arnavon, Cyrille. "*Absalon! Absalon!* et l'histoire." *La révue des lettres modernes* 5 (Winter 1959): 474–97.

Aswell, Duncan. "The Puzzling Design of *Absalom, Absalom!*" *Kenyon Review* 30 (1968): 67–84. Reprinted in Muhlenfeld, *William Faulkner's* Absalom, 93–107.

Atkins, Anselm. "The Matched Halves of *Absalom, Absalom!*" *Modern Fiction Studies* 15 (Summer 1969): 264–65.

Backman, Melvin. *Faulkner, the Major Years: A Critical Study.* Bloomington: Indiana Univ. Press, 1966.

————. "Faulkner's Sick Heroes: Bayard Sartoris and Quentin Compson." *Modern Fiction Studies* 2 (Autumn 1956): 95–108.

————. "Sickness and Primitivism: A Dominant Pattern in Faulkner's Work." *Accent* 14 (Winter 1954): 61–73.

————. "Sutpen and the South: A Study of *Absalom, Absalom!*" *PMLA* 8 (1965): 596–604.

Balakian, Anna. "Relativism in the Arts and the Road to the Absolute." In *Relativism in the Arts.* Edited by Betty Jean Craige, 75–98. Athens: Univ. of Georgia Press, 1983.

Baldanza, Frank. "Faulkner and Stein: A Study in Stylistic Intransigence." *Georgia Review* 13 (Fall 1959): 274–86.

Barth, J. Robert. "Faulkner and the Calvinist Tradition." *Thought* 39 (Spring 1964): 100–120.

Bashiruddin, Zeba. "The Lost Individual in *Absalom, Absalom!*" *American Studies Research Center Newsletter* (Hyderabad) 11 (Dec. 1967): 49–52.

Bassett, John. *William Faulkner: An Annotated Checklist of Recent Criticism.* Kent, Ohio: Kent State Univ. Press, 1983.

Bassett, John E. "*Absalom, Absalom!* The Limits of Narrative Form." *Modern Language Quarterly* 46 (Sept. 1985): 276–92.

Beach, Joseph Warren. *American Fiction, 1920–1940.* New York: Macmillan, 1941.

Beck, Warren. *Faulkner: Essays.* Madison: Univ. of Wisconsin Press, 1976.

————. "Faulkner and the South." *Antioch Review* 1 (Spring 1941): 82–94.

Behrens, Ralph. "Collapse of Dynasty: The Thematic Center of *Absalom, Absalom!*" *PMLA* 89 (1974): 24–33.

Beja, Morris. *Epiphany in the Modern Novel.* Seattle: Univ. of Washington Press, 1971.

Bennett, J. A. W. "Faulkner and A. E. Housman." *Notes and Queries,* n.s. 27 (June 1980): 234.

Berzon, Judith R. *Neither White nor Black: The Mulatto Character in American Fiction*. New York: New York Univ. Press, 1978.

Bjork, Lennart. "Ancient Myths and the Moral Framework of Faulkner's *Absalom, Absalom!*" *American Literature* 35 (1963): 196–204.

Blake, Nancy. "Creation and Procreation: The Voice and the Name, or Biblical Intertextuality in *Absalom, Absalom!* In *Intertextuality in Faulkner*. Edited by Michel Gresset and Noel Polk, 128–43. Jackson: Univ. Press of Mississippi, 1985.

Bleikasten, André. "Fathers in Faulkner." In *The Fictional Father: Lacanian Readings of the Text*. Edited by Robert Con Davis, 135–43. Amherst: Univ. of Massachusetts Press, 1981.

Blotner, Joseph. *Faulkner: A Biography*. New York: Random House, 1974.

Bluestein, Gene. "Faulkner and Miscegenation." *Arizona Quarterly* 43 (Summer 1987): 151–64.

Bond, Virginia O. "The Twining of Wistaria." *DeKalb Literary Arts Journal*, 1984, 19–23.

Bosha, Francis J. "A Source for the Names Charles and Wash in *Absalom, Absalom!*" *Notes on Modern American Literature* 4, Item 13.

Boswell, George. "Epic, Drama, and Faulkner's Fiction." *Kentucky Folklore Record* 25 (Jan.–June 1979): 16–27.

Bradford, M. E. "Brother, Son, Heir: The Structural Focus of Faulkner's *Absalom, Absalom!*" *Sewanee Review* 78 (Jan.–Mar. 1970): 76–98.

Breaden, Dale C. "William Faulkner and the Land." *American Quarterly* 10 (Fall 1958): 344–57.

Breit, Harvey. Introduction to *Absalom, Absalom!* New York: Modern Library, 1951.

Brodsky, Claudia. "The Working of Narrative in *Absalom, Absalom!* A Textual Analysis." *Amerikastudien* 23 (1978): 240–59.

Brooks, Cleanth. "Faulkner and History." *Mississippi Quarterly* 25 (Spring 1972 supplement): 3–14.

———. "Faulkner's Ultimate Values." In *Faulkner and the Southern Renaissance*. Edited by Doreen Fowler and Ann J. Abadie, 266–81. Jackson: Univ. Press of Mississippi, 1982.

———. *The Hidden God*. New Haven: Yale Univ. Press, 1963.

———. "On *Absalom, Absalom!*" *Mosaic* 7 (Fall 1973): 159–83.

———. *On the Prejudices, Predilections, and Firm Beliefs of William Faulkner*. Baton Rouge: Louisiana State Univ. Press, 1987.

———. "The Poetry of Miss Rosa Canfield" [*sic*]. *Shenandoah* 20 (Spring 1970): 199–206.

———. "The Sense of Community in Yoknapatawpha Fiction." *University of Mississippi Studies in English* 15 (1978): 3–18.

————. *A Shaping Joy: Studies in the Writer's Craft.* New York: Harcourt
Brace Jovanovich, 1971.
————. *William Faulkner: The Yoknapatawpha Country.* New Haven: Yale
Univ. Press, 1963.
————. *William Faulkner: Toward Yoknapatawpha and Beyond.* New Ha-
ven: Yale Univ. Press, 1978.
Brooks, Peter. "Incredulous Narration: *Absalom, Absalom!*" *Comparative
Literature* 34 (Summer 1982): 247–68.
Broughton, Panthea Reid. *William Faulkner: The Abstract and the Actual.*
Baton Rouge: Louisiana State Univ. Press, 1974.
Brown, Calvin S. "Faulkner as Aphorist." *Révue de Littérature Comparée*
53 (July–Sept. 1979): 277–98.
Brown, May Cameron, and Esta Seaton. "William Faulkner's Unlikely
Detective: Quentin Compson in *Absalom, Absalom!*" *Essays in Arts
and Sciences* 8 (May 1979): 27–33.
Brown, William R. "Mr. Stark on Mr. Strawson on Referring." *Language
and Style* 7 (Summer 1974): 219–24.
Brumm, Ursula. "Forms and Functions of History in the Novels of Wil-
liam Faulkner." *Archiv für das Studium der Neueren Sprachen und Lit-
eraturen* 209 (Aug. 1972): 43–56.
————. "Thoughts on History and the Novel." *Comparative Literature
Studies* 6 (Sept. 1969): 317–30.
Brylowski, Walter. *Faulkner's Olympian Laugh: Myth in the Novels.* De-
troit: Wayne State Univ. Press, 1968.
Burgum, Edward Berry. *The Novel and the World's Dilemma.* New York:
Oxford Univ. Press, 1963.
Burke, Kenneth. "Fact, Inference, and Proof in the Analysis of Literary
Symbolism." In Conference on Science, Philosophy, and Religion
in Their Relation to the Democratic Way of Life, *Symbols and Values:
An Initial Study.* Edited by Lyman Bryson et al., 283–306. New
York: Harper and Brothers, 1954.
Burns, Stuart L. "Sutpen's 'Incidental' Wives and the Question of Re-
spectability." *Mississippi Quarterly* 30 (Summer 1977): 445–47.
Callen, Shirley. "Planter and Poor White in *Absalom, Absalom!*—'Wash'
and *The Mind of the South.*" *South Central Bulletin* 23 (Winter 1963):
24–36.
Cambon, Glauco. "My Faulkner: The Untranslatable Demon." In *Wil-
liam Faulkner: The Prevailing Verities and World Literature.* Edited by
W. T. Zyla and Wendell M. Aycock, 77–93. Lubbock: Texas Tech
Univ. Press, 1973.
Campbell, Harry Modean. "Faulkner's *Absalom, Absalom!*" *Explicator* 7
(Dec. 1948), Item 24.
————, and Ruel E. Foster. *William Faulkner: A Critical Appraisal.* Norman: Univ. of Oklahoma Press, 1951.

Campbell, Leslie Jean. "Exercises in Doom: Yoknapatawpha County Weddings." *Publications of the Arkansas Philological Association* 4 (1978): 2–7.

Canellas, Maria Isabel Jesus Costa. "Time in Faulkner's *Absalom, Absalom!* as Related to Film Technique." *Estudos Anglo-Americanos* (São Paulo, Brazil) 2 (1978): 33–44.

Canine, Karen McFarland. "The Case Hierarchy and Faulkner's Relatives in *Absalom, Absalom!*" *Southeastern Conference on Linguistics Bulletin* 3, no. 2 (1979): 63–80.

———. "Faulkner's Theory of Relativity: Non-Restrictives in *Absalom, Absalom!*" *Southeastern Conference on Linguistics Review* 5, no. 3 (1981): 118–34.

Chabot, C. Barry. "Faulkner's Rescued Patrimony." *Review of Existential Psychology and Psychiatry* 13 (1974): 274–86.

Chandler, Marilyn R. "The Space Makers: Passive Power in Faulkner's Novels." *College Literature* 15, no. 3 (1988): 281–88.

Chavkin, Allan. "The Imagination as the Alternative to Sutpen's Design." *Arizona Quarterly* 37 (1981): 116–26.

Chikamori, Kazue. "Unity of Theme and Technique in *Absalom, Absalom!*" *Essays and Studies in British and American Literature* (Japan) 11 (Summer 1963): 65–88.

Church, Margaret. *Time and Reality: Studies in Contemporary Fiction.* Chapel Hill: Univ. of North Carolina Press, 1963.

Clark, William Bedford. "The Serpent of Lust in the Southern Garden." *Southern Review* 10 (Autumn 1974): 805–22.

Clark, William G. "Is King David a Racist?" *University Review* (Kansas City) 34 (Dec. 1967): 121–26.

Clarke, Deborah L. "Familiar and Fantastic: Women in *Absalom, Absalom!*" *Faulkner Journal* 2 (Fall 1986): 62–72.

Cleopatra, Sister. "*Absalom, Absalom!* The Failure of the Sutpen Design." *Literary Half-Yearly* 16, no. 1 (1975): 74–93.

Clifford, Paula M. "The American Novel and the French *Nouveau Roman:* Some Linguistic and Stylistic Comparisons." *Comparative Literature Studies* 13 (Dec. 1976): 348–58.

Coanda, Richard. "*Absalom, Absalom!* The Edge of Infinity." *Renascence* 11 (Autumn 1958): 3–9.

Cobley, Evelyn. "Desire and Reciprocal Violence in *Absalom, Absalom!*" *English Studies in Canada* 13 (Dec. 1987): 420–37.

Coffee, Jessie McGuire. *Faulkner's Un-Christlike Christians: Biblical Allusions in the Novels.* Ann Arbor: UMI Research, 1983.

Conley, Timothy K. "Beardsley and Faulkner." *Journal of Modern Literature* 5 (Sept. 1976): 339–56.

Connolly, Thomas E. "Fate and 'The Agony of Will': Determinism in Some Works of William Faulkner." In *Essays on Determinism in Amer-*

ican Literature. Edited by S. J. Krause. Kent Studies in English, no. 1, 36–52. Kent, Ohio: Kent State Univ. Press, 1964.

————. "Point of View in Faulkner's *Absalom, Absalom!*" *Modern Fiction Studies* 27 (Summer 1981): 255–72.

————. "A Skeletal Outline of *Absalom, Absalom!*" *College English* 25 (Nov. 1963): 110–14.

Cook, Albert Spaulding. *The Meaning of Fiction.* Detroit: Wayne State Univ. Press, 1960.

Cook, Richard M. "Popeye, Flem and Sutpen: The Faulknerian Villain as Grotesque." *Studies in American Fiction* 2 (1975): 3–14.

Cornell, Brenda. "Faulkner's 'Evangeline': A Preliminary Stage." *Southern Quarterly* 22 (Summer 1984): 22–41

Cowley, Malcolm. Introduction to *Viking Portable Faulkner.* New York: Viking, 1946.

————. "An Introduction to William Faulkner." In *Critiques and Essays on Modern Fiction.* Edited by John W. Aldridge, 427–46. New York: Ronald, 1952.

————. "Magic in Faulkner." In *Faulkner, Modernism, and Film: Faulkner and Yoknapatawpha, 1978.* Edited by Evans Harrington and Ann J. Abadie, 3–19. Jackson: Univ. Press of Mississippi, 1979.

————. "Poe in Mississippi." *New Republic,* Nov. 4, 1936, 22.

————. "William Faulkner's Legend of the South." *Sewanee Review* 53 (Summer 1945): 343–61.

Cox, James M. Review of *Doubling and Incest / Repetition and Revenge: A Speculative Reading of Faulkner* by John T. Irwin. *MLN* 91 (1976): 1120–31.

Creighton, Joanne V. *William Faulkner's Craft of Revision.* Detroit: Wayne State Univ. Press, 1977.

Culler, Jonathan. *Structuralist Poetics.* Ithaca: Cornell Univ. Press, 1975.

Davenport, Francis Garvin, Jr. *The Myth of Southern History: Historical Consciousness in Twentieth-Century Southern Literature.* Nashville: Vanderbilt Univ. Press, 1970.

Davis, Robert Con. "The Symbolic Father in Yoknapatawpha County." *Journal of Narrative Technique* 10 (Winter 1980): 39–55.

Davis, Thadious M. " 'Be Sutpen's Hundred': Imaginative Projection of Landscape in *Absalom, Absalom!*" *Southern Literary Journal* 13 (Spring 1981): 3–14.

————. "The Yoking of 'Abstract Contradictions': Clytie's Meaning in *Absalom, Absalom!*" *Studies in American Fiction* 7 (Autumn 1979): 209–19.

DeVoto, Bernard. "Witchcraft in Mississippi." *Saturday Review of Literature,* 31 Oct. 1936.

Dickerson, Lynn. "A Possible Source for the Title *Absalom, Absalom!*" *Mississippi Quarterly* 31 (Summer 1978): 423–24.

————. "Thomas Sutpen: Mountain Stereotype in *Absalom, Absalom!*" *Appalachian Heritage* 12 (Spring 1984): 73–78.

Dillingham, William B. "William Faulkner and the 'Tragic Condition.'" *Edda* 66, Heft 5 (1966): 322–35.

Donaldson, Laura E. "The Perpetual Conversation: The Process of Traditioning in *Absalom, Absalom!*" *Modernist Studies: Literature and Culture* 4 (1982): 176–94.

Donaldson, Susan V. "Subverting History: Women and Narrative in *Absalom, Absalom!*" In *Commemorating the Past: Celebrations and Retrospection*. Edited by Don Harkness, vi, 37–40. Tampa: American Studies Press, 1987.

Doody, Terrence. *Confession and Community in the Novel.* Baton Rouge: Louisiana State Univ. Press, 1980.

————. "Shreve McCannon and the Confessions of *Absalom, Absalom!*" *Studies in the Novel, North Texas State* 6 (1974): 454–69.

Doxey, W. S. "Father Time and the Grim Reaper in *Absalom, Absalom!*" *Notes on Contemporary Literature* 8, no. 3 (May 1978): 6–7.

Edmonds, Irene C. "Faulkner and the Black Shadow." In *Southern Renascence: The Literature of the Modern South*. Edited by Louis D. Rubin, Jr., and Robert D. Jacobs, 192–206. Baltimore: Johns Hopkins Univ. Press, 1953.

Edwards, Duane. "Flem Snopes and Thomas Sutpen: Two Versions of Respectability." *Dalhousie Review* 51 (Winter 1972): 559–70.

Egan, Philip J. "Embedded Story Structures in *Absalom, Absalom!*" *American Literature* 55 (1983): 199–214.

Eigner, Edwin M. "Faulkner's Isaac and the American Ishmael." *Jahrbuch für Amerikastudien* 14 (1969): 107–15.

Ellis, John M. *The Theory of Literary Criticism: A Logical Analysis.* Berkeley and Los Angeles: Univ. of California Press, 1974.

Engler, Bernd. "William Faulkner's *Absalom, Absalom!* Five Decades of Critical Reception." *Yearbook of Research in English and American Literature: Berlin* 5 (1987): 221–70.

Fadiman, Clifton. "Faulkner, Extra-special, Double-distilled." *New Yorker,* Oct. 31, 1936, 62–64.

Faulkner, William. *The Sound and the Fury.* New York: Vintage, 1954.

Fiedler, Leslie A. *Love and Death in the American Novel.* New York: Stein and Day, 1966.

Fielding, Henry. *Tom Jones.* New York: Norton, 1973.

Flint, R. W. "Faulkner as Elegist." *Hudson Review* 7 (Summer 1954): 246–57.

Flores, Ralph. *The Rhetoric of Doubtful Authority: Deconstructive Readings of Self-Questioning Narratives, St. Augustine to Faulkner.* Ithaca: Cornell Univ. Press, 1984.

Flynn, Peggy. "The Sister Figure and 'Little Sister Death' in the Fiction of William Faulkner." *University of Mississippi Studies in English* 14 (1976): 99–117.

Ford, Daniel G. "Comments on William Faulkner's Temporal Vision in *Sanctuary, The Sound and the Fury, Light in August, Absalom, Absalom!*" *Southern Quarterly* 15 (Apr. 1977): 283–90.

———. "Maybe Happen Is Never Once: Some Critical Thought on Faulkner's Use of Time." *Publications of the Arkansas Philological Association* 5 (1979): 9–15.

Forrer, Richard. "*Absalom, Absalom!* Story-Telling as a Mode of Transcendence." *Southern Literary Journal* 9 (Fall 1976): 22–46.

Foster, Ruel E. "Social Order and Disorder in Faulkner's Fiction." *Approach* 55 (Spring 1965): 20–28.

Fowler, Doreen. *Faulkner's Changing Vision: From Outrage to Affirmation.* Ann Arbor: UMI Research, 1983.

Friedman, Alan Warren. *William Faulkner.* New York: Ungar, 1984.

Fujihara, Ikuko. "Beyond Closed Doors: Quentin Compson and Isaac McCaslin." In *William Faulkner: Materials, Studies, and Criticism* (Tokyo) 3 (July 1980): 31–43.

———. "From Voice to Silence: Writing in *Absalom, Absalom!*" *Studies in English Literature* (Tokyo), 1984, 75–91.

Gallagher, Susan. "To Love and to Honor: Brothers and Sisters in Faulkner's Yoknapatawpha County." *Essays in Literature* 7 (Fall 1980): 213–44.

Garzilli, Enrico. *Circles without Center: Paths to the Discovery and Creation of Self in Modern Literature.* Cambridge: Harvard Univ. Press, 1972.

Gidley, Mark. "Elements of the Detective Story in William Faulkner's Fiction." *Journal of Popular Culture* 7 (Summer 1973): 97–123.

Giordano, Frank R., Jr. "*Absalom, Absalom!* as a Portrait of the Artist." In *From Irving to Steinbeck: Studies in American Literature in Honor of Harry R. Warfel.* Edited by Motley Deakin and Peter Liscia, 97–107. Gainesville: Univ. of Florida Press, 1972.

Gladstein, Mimi Reisel. *The Indestructible Woman in Faulkner, Hemingway, and Steinbeck.* Ann Arbor: UMI Research, 1986.

Glassman, Steve. "The Influence of Conrad's *Chance* on *Absalom, Absalom!*" *Notes on Mississippi Writers* 15 (1983): 1–4.

Glicksburg, Charles Irving. "William Faulkner and the Negro Problem." *Phylon* 10 (June 1949): 153–60.

———. "The World of William Faulkner." *Arizona Quarterly* 5 (1949): 46–58.

Godden, Richard. "So That's What Frightens Them under the Tree." *Journal of American Studies* 11 (1977): 371–77.

Gold, Joseph. *William Faulkner: A Study in Humanism from Metaphor to Discourse.* Norman: Univ. of Oklahoma Press, 1966.

Goldman, Arnold. "Faulkner's Images of the Past: From *Sartoris* to *The Unvanquished.*" *Yearbook of English Studies* 7 (1978): 109–24.

———. Introduction to *Twentieth-Century Interpretations of* Absalom, Absalom! *A Collection of Critical Essays.* Englewood Cliffs, N.J.: Prentice-Hall, 1971.

Gossett, Louise Y. *Violence in Recent Southern Fiction.* Durham: Duke Univ. Press, 1965.

Gowda, H. H. Anniah. "Visions of Decadence: William Faulkner's *Absalom, Absalom!* and V. S. Naipaul's *The Mimic Men.*" *Literary Half-Yearly* 23, no. 1 (1982): 71–80.

Gray, James D. "Shreve's Lesson of Love: Power of the Unsaid in *Absalom, Absalom!*" *New Orleans Review* 14 (Winter 1987): 24–35.

Gray, Richard. "The Meanings of History: William Faulkner's *Absalom, Absalom!*" *Dutch Quarterly Review of Anglo-American Letters* 3 (1973): 97–110.

Gresset, Michel. *Faulkner and Idealism: Perspectives from Paris.* Jackson: Univ. Press of Mississippi, 1983.

Grimwood, Michael. *Heart in Conflict: Faulkner's Struggles with Vocation.* Athens: Univ. of Georgia Press, 1987.

Guerard, Albert J. "The Faulknerian Voice." In *The Maker and the Myth: Faulkner and Yoknapatawpha, 1977.* Edited by Evans Harrington and Ann J. Abadie, 25–42. Jackson: Univ. Press of Mississippi, 1978.

———. *The Triumph of the Novel: Dickens, Dostoevsky, Faulkner.* New York: Oxford Univ. Press, 1976.

Guetti, James. *The Limits of Metaphor.* Ithaca: Cornell Univ. Press, 1967.

Gwin, Minrose C. *Black and White Women of the Old South.* Knoxville: Univ. of Tennessee Press, 1985.

Gwynn, Frederick L., and Joseph L. Blotner, eds. *Faulkner in the University: Class Conferences at the University of Virginia, 1957–1958.* Charlottesville: Univ. Press of Virginia, 1959.

Hagan, John. "Déjà vu and the Effect of Timelessness in Faulkner's *Absalom, Absalom!*" *Bucknell Review* 11 (1963): 33–52.

———. "Fact and Fancy in *Absalom, Absalom!*" *College English* 24 (Dec. 1962): 215–18.

Hagopian, John V. "*Absalom, Absalom!* and the Negro Question." *Modern Fiction Studies* 19 (Summer 1973): 207–11.

———. "The Biblical Background of Faulkner's *Absalom, Absalom!*" *CEA Critic* 36 (Jan. 1974): 22–24. Reprinted in Muhlenfeld, *William Faulkner's* Absalom, 131–34.

———. "Black Insight in *Absalom, Absalom!*" *Faulkner Studies* 1 (1980): 29–37.

Hall, Constance Hill. *Incest in Faulkner: A Metaphor for the Fall.* Ann Arbor: UMI Research, 1986.

Hammond, Donald. "Faulkner's Levels of Awareness." *Florida Quarterly* 1, no. 2 (1967): 75–78.

Hardy, John E. *Man in the Modern Novel*. Seattle: Univ. of Washington Press, 1964.

Harrington, Evans, and Ann J. Abadie. *The Maker and the Myth: Faulkner and Yoknapatawpha*. Jackson: Univ. Press of Mississippi, 1978.

———. *The South and Faulkner's Yoknapatawpha*. Jackson: Univ. Press of Mississippi, 1977.

Harter, Carol Clancey. "Recent Faulkner Scholarship: Five More Turns of the Screw." *Journal of Modern Literature* 4 (1974): 139–45.

Hartman, Geoffrey. "The Aesthetics of Complicity." *Georgia Review* 28 (Fall 1974): 384–403.

Hartt, Julian N. *The Lost Image of Man*. Baton Rouge: Louisiana State Univ. Press, 1963.

Harvey, W. J. *Character and the Novel*. Ithaca: Cornell Univ. Press, 1965.

Haury, Beth B. "The Influence of Robinson Jeffers' 'Tamar' on *Absalom, Absalom!*" *Mississippi Quarterly* 25 (Summer 1972): 356–58.

Hawkins, E. O. "Faulkner's 'Duke John of Lorraine.'" *American Notes and Queries* 4 (Sept. 1965): 22.

Hayase, Hironori. "*Absalom, Absalom!* The Meaning of Charles Bon's Murder." *Kyushu American Literature* 28 (Oct. 1987): 81–83.

Healy, J. J. "Structuralism Applied: American Literature and Its Subordination to Structure." *Ariel: A Review of International English Literature* 14 (Apr. 1983): 35–51.

Henderson, Harry B., III. *Versions of the Past: The Historical Imagination in American Fiction*. New York: Oxford Univ. Press, 1974.

Herndon, Jerry A. "Faulkner: Meteor, Earthquake, and Sword." In *Faulkner: The Unappeased Imagination, a Collection of Critical Essays*. Edited by Glenn O. Carey, 175–93. Troy, N.Y.: Whitston, 1980.

Hlavsa, Virginia V. "The Vision of the Advocate in *Absalom, Absalom!*" *Novel* 8 (Fall 1974): 51–70.

Hodgson, John A. "'Logical Sequence and Continuity': Some Observations on the Typographical and Structural Consistency of *Absalom, Absalom!*" *American Literature* 43 (1971): 97–107.

Hoffman, A. C. "Faulkner's *Absalom, Absalom!*" *Explicator* 10 (Nov. 1951), Item 12.

———. "Point of View in *Absalom, Absalom!*" *University of Kansas City Review* 19 (Summer 1953): 233–39.

Holder, Alan. *The Imagined Past*. Lewisburg, Pa.: Bucknell Univ. Press, 1980.

Holman, C. Hugh. "*Absalom, Absalom!* The Historian as Detective." *Sewanee Review* 79 (Autumn 1971): 542–53.

———. *The Roots of Southern Writing*. Athens: Univ. of Georgia Press, 1972.

————. *Three Modes of Southern Fiction: Ellen Glasgow, William Faulkner, Thomas Wolfe.* Athens: Univ. of Georgia Press, 1966.

————. "'To Grieve on Universal Bones': The Past as Burden." In *The Immoderate Past: The Southern Writer and History*, 66–92. Athens: Univ. of Georgia Press, 1977.

Holmes, Edward M. *Faulkner's Twice-Told Tales: His Re-use of His Material.* The Hague: Mouton, 1966.

Hopper, Vincent F. "Faulkner's Paradise Lost." *Virginia Quarterly Review* 23 (Summer 1974): 405–20.

Howe, Irving. *William Faulkner: A Critical Study.* New York: Vintage, 1951.

Hunt, John W. "The Disappearance of Quentin Compson." In *Critical Essays on William Faulkner: The Compson Family.* Edited by Arthur F. Kinney, 366–80. Boston: G. K. Hall, 1982.

————. "Keeping the Hoop Skirts Out: Historiography in Faulkner's *Absalom, Absalom!*" *Faulkner Studies* 1 (1980): 38–47.

————. *William Faulkner: Art in Theological Tension.* Syracuse: Syracuse Univ. Press, 1965.

Hunter, Edwin R. *William Faulkner: Narrative Practice and Prose Style.* Washington, D.C.: Windhover, 1973.

Ilacqua, Alma A. "Faulkner's *Absalom, Absalom!* An Aesthetic Projection of the Religious Sense of Beauty." *Ball State University Forum* 21 (Spring 1980): 34–41.

Inscoe, John C. "Faulkner, Race, and Appalachia." *South Atlantic Quarterly* 86, no. 3 (1987): 244–53.

Irwin, John T. *Doubling and Incest / Repetition and Revenge: A Speculative Reading of Faulkner.* Baltimore: Johns Hopkins Univ. Press, 1975.

Isaacs, Neil. "*Götterdämmerung* in Yoknapatawpha." *Tennessee Studies in Literature* 8 (1963): 47–55.

Jackson, Blyden. "Faulkner's Depiction of the Negro." *University of Mississippi Studies in English* 15 (1978): 33–47.

Jackson, Naomi. "Faulkner's Woman: 'Demon-Nun' and 'Angel-Witch.'" *Ball State University Forum* 8 (Winter 1967): 12–20.

Jacobs, Robert D. "Faulkner and the Tragedy of Isolation." In *Southern Renascence: The Literature of the Modern South.* Edited by Louis D. Rubin, Jr., and Robert D. Jacobs, 170–91. Baltimore: Johns Hopkins Univ. Press, 1966.

————. "How Do *You* Read Faulkner?" *Provincial* 1, no. 4 (1957): 3–5.

————. "William Faulkner: The Passion and the Penance." In *South: Modern Southern Literature in Its Cultural Setting.* Edited by Louis D. Rubin, Jr., and Robert D. Jacobs, 142–76. Garden City, N.Y.: Doubleday, 1961.

Jehlen, Myra. *Class and Character in Faulkner's South.* New York: Columbia Univ. Press, 1976.

Jenkins, Lee. "Faulkner, the Mythic Mind, and the Blacks." *Literature and Psychology* 27 (1977): 74–91.

————. *Faulkner and Black-White Relations: A Psychoanalytic Approach.* New York: Columbia Univ. Press, 1981.

Jones, Suzanne W. "*Absalom, Absalom!* and the Custom of Storytelling: A Reflection of Southern Social and Literary History." *Southern Studies* 24 (Spring 1985): 82–112.

Justus, James H. "The Epic Design of *Absalom, Absalom!*" *Texas Studies in Literature and Language* 4 (Summer 1962): 157–76. Reprinted in Muhlenfeld, *William Faulkner's* Absalom, 35–54.

Kapur, Usha. "The Role of Rosa Coldfield in *Absalom, Absalom!*" *Punjab University Research Bulletin* 17 (Oct. 1986): 73–79.

Karl, Frederick R. *William Faulkner: American Writer.* New York: Weidenfeld & Nicolson, 1989.

Kartiganer, Donald M. "Faulkner's *Absalom, Absalom!* The Discovery of Values." *American Literature* 37 (1965): 291–306.

————. *The Fragile Thread: The Meaning of Form in Faulkner's Novels.* Amherst: Univ. of Massachusetts Press, 1979.

————. "Process and Product: A Study in Modern Literary Form, Part II." *Massachusetts Review* 12 (Autumn 1971): 789–816.

————. "Quentin Compson and Faulkner's Drama of the Generations." In *Critical Essays on William Faulkner: The Compson Family.* Edited by Arthur Kinney, 381–401. Boston: G. K. Hall, 1982.

Kauffman, Linda. "Devious Channels of Decorous Ordering: A Lover's Discourse in *Absalom, Absalom!*" *Modern Fiction Studies* 29 (Summer 1983): 183–200.

————. *Discourses of Desire: Gender, Genre, and Epistolary Fictions.* Ithaca: Cornell Univ. Press, 1986.

Kawin, Bruce F. "Faulkner's Film Career: The Years with Hawks." In *Faulkner, Modernism, and Film: Faulkner and Yoknapatawpha, 1978.* Edited by Evans Harrington and Ann J. Abadie. Jackson: Univ. Press of Mississippi, 1979, 163–81.

————. *The Mind of the Novel: Reflexive Fiction and the Ineffable.* Princeton: Princeton Univ. Press, 1982.

————. "The Montage Element in Faulkner's Fiction." In *Faulkner, Modernism, and Film: Faulkner and Yoknapatawpha, 1978.* Edited by Evans Harrington and Ann J. Abadie. Jackson: Univ. Press of Mississippi, 1979, 103–26.

Kellner, R. Scott. "A Reconsideration of Character: Relationships in *Absalom, Absalom!*" *Notes on Mississippi Writers* 7 (1974): 39–43.

Kent, George E. "The Black Woman in Faulkner's Works, with the Exclusion of Dilsey," pt. 2. *Phylon* 36 (Mar. 1975): 55–67.

Kerr, Elizabeth M. "The Evolution of Yoknapatawpha." *University of Mississippi Studies in English* 14 (1976): 23–62.

———. *William Faulkner's Gothic Domain.* Port Washington, N.Y.: Kennikat, 1979.

———. *William Faulkner's Yoknapatawpha: "A Kind of Keystone in the Universe."* New York: Fordham Univ. Press, 1983.

———. "The Women of Yoknapatawpha." *University of Mississippi Studies in English* 15 (1978): 83–100.

———. *Yoknapatawpha: Faulkner's "Little Postage Stamp of Native Soil."* New York: Fordham Univ. Press, 1969.

Kestner, Joseph A. *The Spatiality of the Novel.* Detroit: Wayne State Univ. Press, 1978.

King, Richard H. *A Southern Renaissance: The Cultural Awakening of the American South, 1930–1955.* New York: Oxford Univ. Press, 1980.

Kinney, Arthur F. "Faulkner's Fourteenth Image." *Paintbrush* 2 (1974): 36–43.

———. *Faulkner's Narrative Poetics: Style as Vision.* Amherst: Univ. of Massachusetts Press, 1978.

———. "Form and Function in *Absalom, Absalom!*" *Southern Review* 14 (Autumn 1978): 677–91.

Kirk, Robert W., and Marvin Klotz. *Faulkner's People.* Berkeley and Los Angeles: Univ. of California Press, 1963.

Klotz, Marvin. "The Triumph over Time: Narrative Form in William Faulkner and William Styron." *Mississippi Quarterly* 17 (Winter 1964): 9–20.

Kohler, Dayton. "William Faulkner and the Social Conscience." *College English* 11 (Dec. 1949): 119–27.

Korenman, Joan S. "Faulkner and 'That Undying Mark.'" *Studies in American Fiction* 4 (1976): 81–91.

Kort, Welsey. "Social Time in Faulkner's Fiction." *Arizona Quarterly* 37 (1981): 101–15.

Krause, David. "Opening Pandora's Box: Re-reading Compson's Letter and Faulkner's *Absalom, Absalom!*" *Centennial Review* 30 (Summer 1986): 358–82.

———. "Reading Bon's Letter and Faulkner's *Absalom, Absalom!*" *PMLA* 99 (1984): 225–41.

———. "Reading Shreve's Letters and Faulkner's *Absalom, Absalom!*" *Studies in American Fiction* 11 (1983): 153–69.

Langford, Gerald. *Faulkner's Revision of* Absalom, Absalom! *A Collation of the Book and the Manuscript.* Austin: Univ. of Texas Press, 1971.

LaRocque, Geraldine E. "*A Tale of Two Cities* and *Absalom, Absalom!*" *Mississippi Quarterly* 35 (Summer 1982): 301–4.

Larsen, Eric. "The Barrier of Language: The Irony of Language in Faulkner." *Modern Fiction Studies* 13 (Spring 1967): 19–31.

Lasater, Alice E. "The Breakdown in Communication in the Twentieth-Century Novel." *Southern Quarterly* 12 (Oct. 1973): 1–14.

Leary, Lewis. *William Faulkner of Yoknapatawpha County.* New York: Crowell, 1973.

Lensing, George S. "The Metaphor of Family in *Absalom, Absalom!*" *Southern Review* 11 (Winter 1975): 99–117.

Lenson, David. *Achilles' Choice: Examples of Modern Tragedy.* Princeton: Princeton Univ. Press, 1975.

Leroy, Gaylord C. "Mythopoeic Materials in *Absalom, Absalom!* What Approach for the Marxist Critic?" *Minnesota Review* 17 (1981): 79–95.

Levin, David. "*Absalom, Absalom!* The Problem of Recreating History." In *In Defense of Historical Literature: Essays on American History, Autobiography, Drama and Fiction.* New York: Hill and Wang, 1967, 118–39.

Levins, Lynn Gartrell. *Faulkner's Heroic Design: The Yoknapatawpha Novels.* Athens: Univ. of Georgia Press, 1976.

———. "The Four Narrative Perspectives in *Absalom, Absalom!*" *PMLA* 85 (1970): 35–47.

Liles, Don Merrick. "William Faulkner's *Absalom, Absalom!* An Exegesis of the Homoerotic Configurations in the Novel." In *Literary Visions of Homosexuality.* Edited by Stuart Kellogg. New York: Haworth, 1983, 99–111.

Lind, Ilse Dusoir. "The Design and Meaning of *Absalom, Absalom!*" In *William Faulkner: Three Decades of Criticism.* Edited by Frederick J. Hoffman and Olga W. Vickery. New York: Harcourt Brace Jovanovich, 1963, 278–304.

Longley, John Lewis, Jr. "Thomas Sutpen: The Tragedy of Aspiration." In *William Faulkner: A Collection of Criticism.* Edited by Dean Morgan Schmitter. New York: McGraw-Hill, 1973, 110–21.

———. *The Tragic Mask: A Study of Faulkner's Heroes.* Chapel Hill: Univ. of North Carolina Press, 1963.

Lorch, Thomas M. "Thomas Sutpen and the Female Principle." *Mississippi Quarterly* 20 (Winter, 1966–67): 38–42.

Loughrey, Thomas F. "Aborted Sacrament in *Absalom, Absalom!*" *Four Quarters* 14 (Nov. 1964): 13–21.

Lubarsky, Jared. "The Highest Freedom: A Reconstruction of Faulkner on Race." *William Faulkner: Materials, Studies, and Criticism* (Tokyo) 3 (Apr. 1981): 9–17.

McClennen, Joshua. "*Absalom, Absalom!* and the Meaning of History." *Papers of the Michigan Academy of Arts and Sciences* 42 (1956): 357–69.

McClure, John. "The Syntax of Decadence in *Absalom, Absalom!*" *Minnesota Review* 17 (1981): 96–103.

McDaniel, Linda E. "Designs in *Wuthering Heights* and *Absalom, Absalom!*" *Notes on Mississippi Writers* 19 (1987): 73–80.

McFague, Sallie. *Literature and the Christian Life*. New Haven: Yale Univ. Press, 1966.

McDonald, Walter R. "Coincidence in the Novel: A Necessary Technique." *College English* 29 (Feb. 1968): 373–88.

McHale, Brian. "Change of Dominant from Modernist to Postmodernist Writing." In *Approaching Postmodernism: Papers Presented at a Workshop on Postmodernism*. Edited by Douwe Fokkema and Hans Bertens. Amsterdam and Philadelphia: John Benjamins, 1986, 53–79.

McHaney, Thomas L. *William Faulkner: A Reference Guide*. Boston: G. K. Hall, 1976.

MacKethan, Lucinda Hardwick. "Faulkner's Sons of the Fathers: How to Inherit the Past." In *The Dream of Arcady: Place and Time in Southern Literature*. Baton Rouge: Louisiana State Univ. Press, 1980.

MacLure, Millar. "Allegories of Innocence." *Dalhousie Review* 40 (Summer 1960): 145–56.

McPherson, Karen. "*Absalom, Absalom!* Telling Scratches." *Modern Fiction Studies* 33 (Autumn 1987): 431–50.

Markowitz, Norman. "William Faulkner's 'Tragic Legend': Southern History and *Absalom, Absalom!*" *Minnesota Review* 17 (1981): 104–17.

Marshall, Sarah Latimer. "Fathers and Sons in *Absalom, Absalom!*" *University of Mississippi Studies in English* 8 (1967): 19–29.

Martin, Reginald. "The Quest for Recognition over Reason: Charles Bon's Death-Journey into Mississippi." *South Central Bulletin* 43, no. 4 (1983): 117–20.

Mathews, James W. "The Civil War of 1936: *Gone with the Wind* and *Absalom, Absalom!*" *Georgia Review* 21 (Winter 1967): 462–69.

Matlack, James H. "The Voices of Time: Narrative Structure in *Absalom, Absalom!*" *Southern Review* 15 (Spring 1979): 333–54.

Matthews, John T. *The Play of Faulkner's Language*. Ithaca: Cornell Univ. Press, 1982.

Mayoux, Jean-Jacques. "The Creation of the Real in William Faulkner." In *William Faulkner: Three Decades of Criticism*. Edited by Frederick J. Hoffman and Olga W. Vickery. New York: Harcourt Brace Jovanovich, 1963, 156–73.

Michel, Pierre. "Shreve McCannon: The Outside Voice in *Absalom, Absalom!*" *Dutch Quarterly Review of Anglo-American Letters* 17 (1987): 214–25.

Middleton, John. "Shreve McCannon and Sutpen's Legacy." *Southern Review* 10 (Winter 1974): 115–24.

Miller, Bernice Berger. "William Faulkner's Thomas Sutpen, Quentin Compson, Joe Christmas: A Study of the Hero-Archetype." Ph.D. diss. University of Florida, 1977.

Miller, David M. "Faulkner's Women." *Modern Fiction Studies* 13 (Spring 1967): 3–17.

Miller, Douglas T. "Faulkner and the Civil War: Myth and Reality." *American Quarterly* 15 (Summer 1963): 200–209.

Miller, J. Hillis. "The Two Relativisms: Point of View and Indeterminacy in the Novel *Absalom, Absalom!*" In *Relativism in the Arts*. Edited by Betty Jean Craige. Athens: Univ. of Georgia Press, 1983, 148–70.

Miller, James E. *Quests Surd and Absurd: Essays in American Literature*. Chicago: Univ. of Chicago Press, 1967.

Millgate, Michael. *The Achievement of William Faulkner*. New York: Random House, 1966.

———. " 'A Cosmos of My Own': The Evolution of Yoknapatawpha." *Fifty Years of Yoknapatawpha: Faulkner and Yoknapatawpha, 1979*. Edited by Doreen Fowler and Ann J. Abadie. Jackson: Univ. Press of Mississippi, 1980, 23–43.

———. "Faulkner and History." In *The South and Faulkner's Yoknapatawpha: The Actual and the Apocryphal*. Edited by Evans Harrington and Ann J. Abadie. Jackson: Univ. Press of Mississippi, 1977, 22–39.

———. " 'The Firmament of Man's History': Faulkner's Treatment of the Past." *Mississippi Quarterly* 25 (Spring 1972 supplement): 25–35.

Milum, Richard A. "Faulkner and the Cavalier Tradition: The French Bequest." *American Literature* 45 (January 1974): 580–89.

Miner, Ward L. *The World of William Faulkner*. New York: Cooper Square, 1963.

Minter, David. "Family, Region, and Myth in Faulkner's Fiction." In *Faulkner and the Southern Renaissance*. Edited by Doreen Fowler and Ann J. Abadie. Jackson: Univ. Press of Mississippi, 1982, 182–203.

———. *The Interpreted Design as a Structural Principle in American Prose*. New Haven: Yale Univ. Press, 1969.

———. " 'Truths More Intense than Knowledge': Notes on Faulkner and Creativity." In *Faulkner and the Southern Renaissance*. Edited by Doreen Fowler and Ann J. Abadie. Jackson: Univ. Press of Mississippi, 1982, 245–65.

———. *William Faulkner: His Life and Work*. Baltimore: Johns Hopkins Univ. Press, 1980.

Moloney, Michael Francis. "The Enigma of Time: Proust, Virginia Woolf, and Faulkner." *Thought* 32 (Spring 1957): 69–85.

Monaghan, David M. "Faulkner's *Absalom, Absalom!*" *Explicator* 31 (Dec. 1972), Item 28.

Montauzon, Christine de. *Faulkner's Absalom, Absalom! and Interpretability: The Inexplicable Unseen*. Berne: Peter Lang, 1985.

Monteiro, George. "The Limits of Professionalism: A Sociological Approach to Faulkner, Fitzgerald and Hemingway." *Criticism* 15 (1973): 145–55.

Mortimer, Gail L. *Faulkner's Rhetoric of Loss: A Study in Perception and Meaning.* Austin: Univ. of Texas Press, 1983.

Muehl, Lois. "Faulkner's Humor in Three Novels and One 'Play.'" *Library Chronicle* 24 (Spring 1968): 78–93.

Muhlenfeld, Elisabeth S. "Shadows with Substance and Ghosts Exhumed: The Women of *Absalom, Absalom!*" *Mississippi Quarterly* 25 (Summer 1972): 289–304.

———. " 'We Have Waited Long Enough': Judith Sutpen and Charles Bon." *Southern Review* 14 (Winter 1978): 66–80.

———. *William Faulkner's* Absalom, Absalom! *A Critical Casebook.* New York: Garland, 1984.

Muller, Christopher. "On William Faulkner's Manner of Narration." *Kwartalnik Neofilologiczny* 25 (1978): 201–12.

Narain, S. K. "*Absalom, Absalom!* by William Faulkner: An Interpretation." *Literary Criterion* 6 (Summer 1964): 116–22.

Nelson, David W. "Two Novels of Speculation: William Faulkner's *Absalom, Absalom!* and Uwe Johnson's *Mutmassungen über Jakob.*" *Papers in Romance* (Seattle) 2, supplement 1 (1980): 51–57.

Newby, Richard L. "Matthew Arnold, the North, and *Absalom, Absalom!*" *American Notes and Queries* 16 (Mar. 1978): 105.

Nilon, Charles H. *Faulkner and the Negro.* New York: Citadel, 1965.

Nishiyama, Tamotsu. "The Structure of *Absalom, Absalom!*" *Kyushu American Literature* (Fukuoka, Japan) 1 (June 1958): 9–13.

O'Brien, Matthew C. "A Note on Faulkner's Civil War Women." *Notes on Mississippi Writers* 1 (1968): 56–63.

O'Connor, William Van. "Faulkner's Legend of the Old South." *Western Humanities Review* 7 (Autumn 1953): 293–301.

———. "Protestantism in Yoknapatawpha County." In *Southern Renascence: The Literature of the Modern South.* Edited by Louis D. Rubin, Jr., and Robert D. Jacobs. Baltimore: Johns Hopkins Univ. Press, 1953, 153–69.

———. *The Tangled Fire of William Faulkner.* New York: Gordian, 1968.

———. *William Faulkner.* Minneapolis: Univ. of Minnesota Press, 1964.

———. O'Donnell, George Marion. "Faulkner's Mythology." In *William Faulkner: Three Decades of Criticism.* Edited by Frederick J. Hoffman and Olga W. Vickery. New York: Harcourt Brace Jovanovich, 1963, 82–93.

O'Donnell, Patrick. "Sub Rosa: Voice, Body, and History in *Absalom, Absalom!*" *College Literature* 15, no. 1 (1989): 28–47.

Ohki Masako. "The Technique of Handling Time in *Absalom, Absalom!*" *Kyushu American Literature* (Fukuoka, Japan) 15 (1974): 89–94.

Onoe, Masaji. "Some T. S. Eliot Echoes in Faulkner." *William Faulkner: Materials, Studies, and Criticism* (Tokyo) 3 (July 1980): 1–15.

Oriard, Michael. "The Ludic Vision of William Faulkner." *Modern Fiction Studies* 28 (Summer 1982): 169–87.

Oswell, D. "The Puzzling Design of *Absalom, Absalom!*" *Kenyon Review* 30 (Winter 1968): 65–84.

Otten, Terry. "Faulkner's Use of the Past: A Comment." *Renascence* 20 (Summer 1968).

Owens, Clarke. "Faulkner's *Absalom, Absalom!*" *Explicator* 42 (Spring 1984): 45–46.

Paddock, Lisa. " 'Trifles with a Tragic Profundity': The Importance of 'Mistral.' " *Mississippi Quarterly* 32 (Summer 1978): 413–22.

Page, Sally R. *Faulkner's Women: Characterization and Meaning*. Deland, Fl.: Everett / Edwards, 1972.

Palumbo, Donald. "The Concept of God in Faulkner's *Light in August, The Sound and the Fury, As I Lay Dying,* and *Absalom, Absalom!*" *South Central Bulletin* 34 (Winter 1979): 142–46.

Parker, Herschel. "What Quentin Saw 'Out There.' " *Mississippi Quarterly* 27 (Summer 1974): 323–26.

Parker, Robert Dale. "The Chronology and Genealogy of *Absalom, Absalom!* The Authority of Fiction and the Fiction of Authority." *Studies in American Fiction* 14 (Autumn 1986): 191–98.

———. *Faulkner and the Novelistic Imagination*. Urbana: Univ. of Illinois Press, 1985.

Parkinson-Zamora, Lois. "The End of Innocence: Myth and Narrative Structure in Faulkner's *Absalom, Absalom!* and García Márquez' *Cien años de soledad. Hispanic Journal* 4 (Fall 1982): 23–40.

Parr, Susan Resneck. "The Fourteenth Image of the Blackbird: Another Look at Truth in *Absalom, Absalom!*" *Arizona Quarterly* 35 (1979): 153–64.

Paterson, John. "Hardy, Faulkner, and the Prosaics of Tragedy." *Centennial Review* 5 (1961): 160–75. In *Twentieth-Century Interpretations of Absalom, Absalom! A Collection of Critical Essays*. Edited by Arnold Goldman. Englewood Cliffs, N.J.: Prentice-Hall, 1971, 32–41.

Payne, Ladell. *Black Novelists and the Southern Literary Tradition*. Athens: Univ. of Georgia Press, 1981.

Pearce, Richard. "Reeling through Faulkner: Pictures of Motion, Pictures in Motion." *Modern Fiction Studies* 24 (Winter 1978–79): 483–95.

Pearson, Norman Holmes. "The American Writer and the Feeling for Community." *English Studies* 43 (Oct. 1962): 403–12.

Peters, Erskine. *William Faulkner: The Yoknapatawpha World and Black Being*. Darby, Pa.: Norwood Editions, 1983.

Petesch, Donald A. "Faulkner on Negroes: The Conflict between the Public Man and the Private Art." *Southern Humanities Review* 10 (1976): 55–64.

Piacentino, Edward J. "Another Possible Source for *Absalom, Absalom!*" *Notes on Mississippi Writers* 10 (1977): 87–93.

Pikoulis, John. *The Art of William Faulkner.* London: Macmillan, 1982.

Pilkington, John. *The Heart of Yoknapatawpha.* Jackson: Univ. Press of Mississippi, 1981.

Pinsker, Sanford. "Thomas Sutpen and Milly Jones: A Note on Paternal Design in *Absalom, Absalom!*" *Notes on Modern American Literature* 1, no. 1 (1976): 6.

Pitavy, François. "The Gothicism of *Absalom, Absalom!* Rosa Coldfield Revisited." In *"A Cosmos of My Own": Faulkner and Yoknapatawpha, 1980.* Edited by Doreen Fowler and Ann J. Abadie. Jackson: Univ. Press of Mississippi, 1981, 199–226.

Poirier, Richard. " 'Strange Gods' in Jefferson, Mississippi: Analysis of *Absalom, Absalom!*" In *William Faulkner: Two Decades of Criticism.* Edited by Frederick J. Hoffman and Olga W. Vickery. East Lansing: Michigan State College Press, 1951, 217–43. Reprinted in Muhlenfeld, *William Faulkner's* Absalom, 1–22.

Polek, Fran James. "The Fourteenth Blackbird: Reflective Deflection in *Absalom, Absalom!*" *University of Portland Review* 28 (Spring 1976): 23–32.

———. "From Renegade to Solid Citizen: The Extraordinary Individual and the Community." *South Dakota Review* 15 (Spring 1977): 61–72.

Polk, Noel. "The Manuscript of *Absalom, Absalom!*" *Mississippi Quarterly* 25 (Summer 1972): 359–67.

Porter, Carolyn. *Seeing and Being: The Plight of the Participant Observer in Emerson, James, Adams and Faulkner.* Middletown, Conn.: Wesleyan Univ. Press, 1981.

Powers, Lyall H. *Faulkner's Yoknapatawpha Comedy.* Ann Arbor: Univ. of Michigan Press, 1980.

Price, Steve. "Shreve's Bon in *Absalom, Absalom!*" *Mississippi Quarterly* 39, no. 3 (1986): 325–35.

Putzel, Max. "What Is Gothic about *Absalom, Absalom!?*" *Southern Literary Journal* 4 (Fall 1971): 3–19.

Radlof, Bernhard. "*Absalom, Absalom!* An Ontological Approach to Sutpen's 'Design.'" *Mosaic* 19 (Winter 1986): 45–56.

Ragan, David Paul. " 'That Tragedy Is Second-Hand': Quentin, Henry, and the Ending of *Absalom, Absalom!*" *Mississippi Quarterly* 39, no. 3 (1986): 337–50.

———. *William Faulkner's* Absalom, Absalom! *A Critical Study.* Ann Arbor: UMI Research, 1987.

Randel, Fred V. "Parentheses in Faulkner's *Absalom, Absalom!*" *Style* 5 (1971): 70–87.

Raper, J. R. "Meaning Called to Life: Alogical Structure in *Absalom, Absalom!*" *Southern Humanities Review* 5 (Winter 1971): 9–23.

Redekop, Magdalene. "*Absalom, Absalom!* through the Spectacles of Shreve McCannon." *William Faulkner: Materials, Studies, and Criticism* (Tokyo) 5 (August 1983): 17–45.

Reed, Joseph W., Jr. *Faulkner's Narrative*. New Haven: Yale Univ. Press, 1973.

Ricks, Beatrice. *William Faulkner: A Bibliography of Secondary Works*. Metuchen, N.J.: Scarecrow, 1981.

Rimmon-Kenan, Shlomith. "From Reproduction to Production: The Status of Narration in Faulkner's *Absalom, Absalom!*" *Degrès* 6 (1978): f–f19.

Rinaldi, Nicholas M. "Game Imagery in Faulkner's *Absalom, Absalom!*" *Connecticut Review* 4, no. 1 (1970): 73–79.

Ringold, Francine. "The Metaphysics of Yoknapatawpha County: Airy Space and Scope for Your Delirium." *Hartford Studies in Literature* 8 (1976): 223–40.

Rio-Jelliffe, R. "*Absalom, Absalom!* as Self-reflexive Novel." *Journal of Narrative Technique* 11 (Spring 1981): 75–90.

Robbins, Deborah. "Desperate Eloquence of *Absalom, Absalom!*" *Mississippi Quarterly* 34 (Summer 1981): 315–24.

Robin, Régine. "*Absalom, Absalom!*" In *Le blanc et le noir chez Melville et Faulkner*. Edited by Viola Sachs. Paris: Mouton, 1974, 67–129.

Rodewald, F. A. "Faulkner's Possible Use of *The Great Gatsby*." *Fitzgerald-Hemingway Annual* (1975): 97–101.

Rodnon, Stewart. "*The House of Seven Gables* and *Absalom, Absalom!*" *Studies in the Humanities* (Indiana, Pa.) 1 (Winter 1969): 42–46.

Rollyson, Carl E., Jr. "*Absalom, Absalom!* The Novel as Historiography." *Literature and History* 5 (Spring 1977): 42–54. Reprinted in Muhlenfeld, *William Faulkner's* Absalom, 157–72.

———. "Faulkner and Historical Fiction: *Redgauntlet* and *Absalom, Absalom!*" *Dalhousie Review* 56 (1976–77): 671–81.

———. "Quentin Durward and Quentin Compson: The Romantic Standard-bearers of Scott and Faulkner." *Massachusetts Studies in English* 7 (1980): 34–39.

———. *Uses of the Past in the Novels of William Faulkner*. Ann Arbor: UMI Research, 1984.

Rome, Joy J. "Love and Wealth in *Absalom, Absalom!*" *Unisa English Studies* 9 (1971): 3–10.

Rose, Maxine. "Echoes of the King James Bible in the Prose Style of *Absalom, Absalom!*" *Arizona Quarterly* 37 (1981): 137–48.

———. "From Genesis to Revelation: The Grand Design of William Faulkner's *Absalom, Absalom!*" *Studies in American Fiction* 8 (1980): 219–28.

Rosenman, John B. "Anderson's *Poor White* and Faulkner's *Absalom, Absalom!*" *Mississippi Quarterly* 29 (Summer 1976): 437–38.

————. "A Matter of Choice: The Locked Door Theme in Faulkner." *South Atlantic Bulletin* 41 (May 1976): 8–12.

Rosenzweig, Paul. "The Narrative Frames in *Absalom, Absalom!* Faulkner's Involuted Commentary on Art." *Arizona Quarterly* 35 (1979): 135–52.

Ross, Stephen M. "Conrad's Influences on Faulkner's *Absalom, Absalom!*" *Studies in American Fiction* 2 (1974): 199–209.

————. "The Evocation of Voice in *Absalom, Absalom!*" *Essays in Literature* 8 (Fall 1981): 135–49.

————. "Faulkner's *Absalom, Absalom!* and the David Story: A Speculative Contemplation." In *The David Myth in Western Literature.* Edited by Raymond-Jean Frontain and Jan Wojcik. West Lafayette, Ind.: Purdue Univ. Press, 1980, 136–53.

————. "Oratory and the Dialogical in *Absalom, Absalom!*" In *Intertextuality in Faulkner.* Edited by Michel Gresset and Noel Polk. Jackson: Univ. Press of Mississippi, 1985, 73–86.

————. " 'Voice' in Narrative Texts: The Example of *As I Lay Dying.*" *PMLA* 94 (1979): 300–310.

Rouberol, Jean. "Faulkner et l'histoire." *RANAM: Recherches Anglaises et Américaines* 9 (1976): 7–17.

Roudiez, Leon S. "*Absalom, Absalom!* The Significance of Contradictions." *Minnesota Review* 17 (1981): 58–78.

Roueché, Berton. "*Absalom, Absalom!*" *University Review* (Kansas City) 3 (Winter 1936): 137–38.

Rubin, Louis D., Jr. *Faraway Country: Writers of the Modern South.* Seattle: Univ. of Washington Press, 1963.

————. "Looking Backward." *New Republic,* Oct. 19, 1974, 20–22.

————. "Scarlett O'Hara and the Two Quentin Compsons." In *The South and Faulkner's Yoknapatawpha: The Actual and the Apocryphal.* Edited by Evans Harrington and Ann J. Abadie. Jackson: Univ. Press of Mississippi, 1977, 168–94.

————. *The Teller and the Tale.* Seattle: Univ. of Washington Press, 1967.

————. "William Faulkner: The Discovery of a Man's Vocation." In *Faulkner: Fifty Years after* The Marble Faun. Edited by George H. Wolfe. University: Univ. of Alabama Press, 1976, 43–68.

————. *The Writer in the South.* Athens: Univ. of Georgia Press, 1972.

Rudich, Norman. "Faulkner and the Sin of Private Property." *Minnesota Review* 17 (1981): 55–57.

Ruppersburg, Hugh M. *Voice and Eye in Faulkner's Fiction.* Athens: Univ. of Georgia Press, 1983.

Sabiston, Elizabeth. "Women, Blacks, and Sutpen's Mythopoeic Drive in *Absalom, Absalom!*" *Modernist Studies: Literature and Culture,* 1, no. 3 (1974–75): 15–26.

Sachs, Viola. *The Myth of America: Essays in the Structures of Literary Imagination*. The Hague: Mouton, 1973.

St. Clair, Janet. "The Refuge of Death: Silencing the Struggles of a Hungry Heart." *Arizona Quarterly* 43 (Summer 1987): 101–18.

Samway, Patrick, S. J. "Storytelling and the Library Scene in Faulkner's *Absalom, Absalom!*" *William Faulkner: Materials, Studies, and Criticism* 2 (1979): 1–20.

Scherer, Olga. "La Contestation du jugement sur pièces chez Dostoievski et Faulkner." *Delta*, Nov. 1976, 47–59.

———. "Faulkner et la fratricide: pour une théorie des titres dans la littérature." *Etudes Anglaises* 30 (July–Sept. 1977): 329–36.

———. "A Polyphonic Insert: Charles's Letter to Judith." In *Intertextuality in Faulkner*. Edited by Michel Gresset and Noel Polk. Jackson: Univ. Press of Mississippi, 1985, 168–177.

———. "Rosie Coldfield et Vanka Karamozov: Le diminutif au service de l'ambivalence." *Révue de Littérature Comparée* 53 (July–Sept. 1979): 311–22.

Schmidtberger, Loren F. "*Absalom, Absalom!* What Clytie Knew." *Mississippi Quarterly* 35 (Summer 1982): 255–63.

———. "Names in *Absalom, Absalom!*" *American Literature* 55 (1983): 83–88.

Schoenberg, Estella. *Old Tales and Talking: Quentin Compson in William Faulkner's* Absalom, Absalom! *and Related Works*. Jackson: Univ. of Mississippi Press, 1977.

Scholes, Robert E. "The Modern American Novel and the Mason-Dixon Line." *Georgia Review* 14 (Summer 1960): 193–204.

———, and Robert Kellogg. *The Nature of Narrative*. New York: Oxford Univ. Press, 1966.

Schrank, Bernice. "Patterns of Reversal in *Absalom, Absalom!*" *Dalhousie Review* 54 (1974–75): 648–66.

Schrero, Elliott M. "*Another Country* and the Sense of Self." *Black Academy Review* 2 (Spring–Summer 1971): 91–100.

Schultz, William J. "Just like Father: Mr. Compson as Cavalier Romancer in *Absalom, Absalom!*" *Kansas Quarterly* 14 (Spring 1982): 115–23.

Schwartz, Lawrence H. *Creating Faulkner's Reputation: The Politics of Modern Literary Criticism*. Knoxville: Univ. of Tennessee Press, 1988.

Scott, Arthur L. "The Faulknerian Sentence." *Prairie Schooner* 27 (Spring 1953): 91–98.

———. "The Myriad Perspectives of *Absalom, Absalom!*" *American Quarterly* 6 (Fall 1954): 210–20. Reprinted in Muhlenfeld, *William Faulkner's* Absalom, 23–34.

Sederberg, Peter C. "Faulkner, Naipaul, and Zola: Violence and the Novel." In *The Artist and Political Vision.* Edited by Benjamin R. Barber and Michael J. Gargas McGrath. New Brunswick, N.J.: Transaction, 1982, 291–315.

Seiden, Melvin. "Faulkner's Ambiguous Negro." *Massachusetts Review* 4 (Summer 1963): 675–90.

Serafin, Joan M. *Faulkner's Use of the Classics.* Ann Arbor: UMI Research, 1983.

Sewall, Richard B. *The Vision of Tragedy.* New Haven: Yale Univ. Press, 1959.

Shirley, William. "The Question of Sutpen's 'Innocence.'" *Southern Literary Messenger* 1, no. 1 (1975): 31–37.

Simpson, Lewis P. "The Fable of the Writer in Southern Fiction." *Prospects* 7 (1982): 249–66.

Singal, Daniel Joseph. *The War Within: From Victorian to Modernist Thought in the South, 1919–1945.* Chapel Hill: Univ. of North Carolina Press, 1982.

Singleton, Marvin K. "Personae at Law and in Equity: The Unity of Faulkner's *Absalom, Absalom!*" *Papers on Language and Literature* 3 (Fall 1967): 354–70.

Skaggs, Merrill Maguire. *The Folk in Southern Fiction.* Athens: Univ. of Georgia Press, 1972.

Slabey, Robert M. "Faulkner's 'Waste Land': Vision in *Absalom, Absalom!*" *Mississippi Quarterly* 14 (Summer 1961): 153–61.

———. "Quentin Compson's 'Lost Childhood.'" *Studies in Short Fiction* 1 (Spring 1964): 173–83.

Slatoff, Walter J. *Quest for Failure.* Ithaca: Cornell Univ. Press, 1960.

Slattery, Dennis Patrick. "And Who to Know: Monuments, Text, and the Trope of Time in *Absalom, Absalom!*" *New Orleans Review* 4 (Winter 1987): 42–51.

———. "Faulkner and His Critics: A General Introduction." *New Orleans Review* 4 (Winter 1987): 5–8.

Snead, James A. *Figures of Division: William Faulkner's Major Novels.* New York: Methuen, 1986.

———. "The 'Joint of Racism': Withholding the Black in *Absalom, Absalom!*" In *William Faulkner's Absalom, Absalom!* Edited by Harold Bloom. New York: Chelsea, 1987, 129–41.

Sowder, William J. "Colonel Thomas Sutpen as Existentialist Hero." *American Literature* 33 (1962): 485–99.

Spivey, Ted R. *The Journey beyond Tragedy: A Study of Myth and Modern Fiction.* Orlando: Univ. Presses of Florida, 1980.

Stafford, William T. *Books Speaking to Books: A Contextual Approach to American Fiction.* Chapel Hill: Univ. of North Carolina Press, 1981.

Stark, John. "The Implications for Stylistics of Strawson's 'On Referring,' with *Absalom, Absalom!* as an Example." *Language and Style* 6 (Fall 1973): 273–80.

Steene, Birgitta. "William Faulkner and the Myth of the American South." *Moderna Språk* 54, no. 3, 270–79.

Steinberg, Aaron. "*Absalom, Absalom!* The Irretrievable Bon." *College Language Association Journal* 9 (Sept. 1965): 61–67.

Steiner, George. Leslie Stephen Memorial Lecture, Cambridge University, Nov. 1, 1985. Partial text pub. in *TLS*, 8 Nov. 1985. Complete text forthcoming from Cambridge Univ. Press.

Sternberg, Meir. "Temporal Ordering, Modes of Expositional Distribution, and Three Models of Rhetorical Control in the Narrative Text: Faulkner, Balzac and Austen." *PTL: Journal for Descriptive Poetics and Theory* 1 (1976): 295–316.

Stewart, David H. "*Absalom* Reconsidered." *University of Toronto Quarterly* 30 (Oct. 1960): 31–44.

Stonum, Gary Lee. *Faulkner's Career: An Internal Literary History.* Ithaca: Cornell Univ. Press, 1979.

Straumann, Heinrich. "Black and White in Faulkner's Fiction." *English Studies* 60 (1979): 462–70.

Sullivan, Walter. "The Decline of Myth in Southern Fiction." *Southern Review* 12 (Winter 1976): 16–31.

———. "Southern Novelists and the Civil War." In *Southern Renascence: The Literature of the Modern South.* Edited by Louis D. Rubin, Jr., and Robert D. Jacobs. Baltimore: Johns Hopkins Univ. Press, 1953, 112–25.

———. "The Tragic Design of *Absalom, Absalom!*" *South Atlantic Quarterly* 50 (Oct. 1951): 552–56.

Sundquist, Eric J. *Faulkner: The House Divided.* Baltimore: Johns Hopkins Univ. Press, 1983.

Swartzlander, Susan. "'That Meager and Fragile Thread': The Artist as Historian in *Absalom, Absalom!*" *Southern Studies* 25 (Spring 1986): 111–19.

Swiggart, Peter. *The Art of Faulkner's Novels.* Austin: Univ. of Texas Press, 1962.

Swink, Helen. "William Faulkner: The Novelist as Oral Narrator." *Georgia Review* 26 (Summer 1976): 183–209.

Sykes, S. W. "The Novel as Conjuration: *Absalom, Absalom!* and *La Route des Flandres.*" *Révue de Littérature Comparée* 53 (1979): 348–57.

Taylor, Walter. "Faulkner's Curse." *Arizona Quarterly* 28 (1972): 333–38.

———. *Faulkner's Search for a South.* Urbana: Univ. of Illinois Press, 1983.

Tebbetts, Terrell L. "Ogre and Pigmies: Sutpen's Stature in *Absalom, Absalom!*" *New Orleans Review* 4 (Winter 1987): 15–23.

Thomas, Douglas M. "Memory-Narrative in *Absalom, Absalom!*" *Faulkner Studies* 2 (Summer 1953): 19–22.

Thompson, Lawrance R. "A Defense of Difficulties in William Faulkner's Art." *Carrell* 4 (Dec. 1963): 7–16.

———. *William Faulkner: An Introduction and Interpretation*. New York: Barnes and Noble, 1963.

Tindall, William York. *The Literary Symbol*. Bloomington: Indiana Univ. Press, 1955.

Tobin, Patricia Drechsel. *Time and the Novel: The Genealogical Imperative*. Princeton: Princeton Univ. Press, 1978.

———. "The Time of Myth and History in *Absalom, Absalom!*" *American Literature* 45 (1973): 252–70.

Todorov, Tzvetan. "All against Humanity." *TLS*, Oct. 4, 1985.

Torsney, Cheryl B. "The Vampire Motif in *Absalom, Absalom!*" *Southern Review* 20 (Summer 1984): 562–69.

Turner, Joseph W. "The Kinds of Historical Fiction." *Genre* 12 (1979): 333–55.

Tuso, Joseph F. "Faulkner's 'Wash.'" *Explicator* 27 (Nov. 1968), Item 17.

Uroff, Margaret Dickie. "The Fictions of *Absalom, Absalom!*" *Studies in the Novel* 11 (Winter 1979): 431–45.

Van Nostrand, A. D. *Everyman His Own Poet*. New York: McGraw-Hill, 1968.

Vande Kieft, Ruth M. "Faulkner's Defeat of Time." *Southern Review* 6 (Autumn 1970): 1100–1109.

Vanderwerken, David L. "Who Killed Jay Gatsby?" *Notes on Modern American Literature* 3 (Spring 1981), Item 12.

Vickery, Olga W. *The Novels of William Faulkner*. Baton Rouge: Louisiana State Univ. Press, 1959.

Volpe, Edmond L. *A Reader's Guide to William Faulkner*. New York: Noonday, 1964.

Wad, Soren. "II—*Absalom, Absalom!*" In *Six American Novels: From New Deal to New Frontier: A Workbook*. Edited by Jens Bøgh and Steffen Skovman. Aarhaus: Akademisk Boghandel, n.d., 96–118.

Wadlington, Warwick. *Reading Faulknerian Tragedy*. Ithaca: Cornell Univ. Press, 1987.

Waggoner, Hyatt. "The Historical Novel and the Southern Past: The Case of *Absalom, Absalom!*" *Southern Literary Journal* 2 (Spring 1970): 69–85.

———. *William Faulkner: From Jefferson to the World*. Lexington: Univ. of Kentucky Press, 1959.

Wagner, Linda Welshimer. *Hemingway and Faulkner: Inventors/Masters*. Metuchen, N.J.: Scarecrow, 1975.

Walters, P. S. "Hallowed Ground: Group Areas in the Structure and Theme of *Absalom, Absalom!*" *Theoria* 47 (1976): 35–55.

Warren, Robert Penn. "Faulkner: The South and the Negro." *Southern Review* 1 (July 1965): 501–29.

Watkins, Evan. *The Critical Act: Criticism and Community*. New Haven: Yale Univ. Press, 1978.

———. "The Politics of Literary Criticism." *Boundary 2* 8 (Fall 1979): 31–38.

Watkins, Floyd C. *The Flesh and the Word: Eliot, Hemingway, Faulkner*. Nashville: Vanderbilt Univ. Press, 1971.

———. "What Happens in *Absalom, Absalom!*" *Modern Fiction Studies* 13 (Spring 1967): 79–87. Reprinted in Muhlenfeld, *William Faulkner's Absalom*, 55–64.

Watson, James G. "Faulkner: Short Story Structures and Reflexive Forms." *Mosaic* 11 (Summer 1978): 127–37.

———. " 'If *Was* Existed': Faulkner's Prophets and the Patterns of History." *Modern Fiction Studies* 21 (Winter 1975–76): 499–507.

Weatherby, H. L. "Sutpen's Garden." *Georgia Review* 21 (Fall 1967): 354–69.

Weinstein, Arnold L. *Vision and Response in Modern Fiction*. Ithaca: Cornell Univ. Press, 1974.

Weinstein, Philip M. "Precarious Sanctuaries: Protection and Exposure in Faulkner's Fiction." *Studies in American Fiction* 6 (1978): 173–91.

Weisgerber, Jean. *Faulkner and Dostoevsky*. Athens: Ohio Univ. Press, 1974.

———. "Faulkner's Monomaniacs: Their Indebtedness to Raskolnikov." *Comparative Literature Studies* 5 (June 1968): 181–93.

Whan, Edgar W. "*Absalom, Absalom!* as Gothic Myth." *Perspective* 3 (Autumn 1950): 192–201.

Wigley, Joseph A. "Imagery and the Interpreter." In *Studies in Interpretation*. Edited by Esther M. Doyle and Virginia H. Floyd. Amsterdam: Rodopi, 1972, 171–90.

Williams, J. Gary. "Quentin Finally Sees Miss Rosa." *Criticism* 21 (1979): 331–46.

Williams, Philip. "Faulkner's Satan Sutpen and the Tragedy of *Absalom, Absalom!*" *Tohuko Gakuin University Review: Essays and Studies in English Language and Literature* 45–46 (Winter 1964): 179–99.

Wilson, Mary Ann T. "Search for an Eternal Present: *Absalom, Absalom!* and *All the King's Men*." *Connecticut Review* 8, no. 1 (1974): 95–100.

Wittenberg, Judith Bryant. *Faulkner: The Transfiguration of Biography*. Lincoln: Univ. of Nebraska Press, 1979.

———. "Faulkner and Eugene O'Neill." *Mississippi Quarterly* 33 (1980): 327–41.

Woodward, Robert H. "Poe's Raven, Faulkner's Sparrow, and Another Window." *Poe Newsletter* 2, no. 1–2 (1969): 37–38.

Young, Thomas Daniel. "Narration as Creative Art: The Role of Quentin Compson in *Absalom, Absalom!*" In *Faulkner, Modernism, and Film.* Edited by Evans Harrington and Ann J. Abadie. Jackson: Univ. Press of Mississippi, 1979, 82–102.

Yu, Beong-Cheon. "Quentin's Troubled Vision." *English Language and Literature* 18 (Summer 1966): 112–19.

Zink, Karl E. "William Faulkner: Form as Experience." *South Atlantic Quarterly* 53 (July 1954): 384–403.

Zoellner, Robert H. "Faulkner's Prose Style in *Absalom, Absalom!*" *American Literature* 30 (1959): 486–502.

Index